MOUNTAIN SAGE

MOUNTAIN SAGE

*The Life Story of Carl Sharsmith,
Yosemite Ranger/Naturalist*

*by
Elizabeth Stone O'Neill*

Yosemite Association
Yosemite National Park, California

Also by Elizabeth Stone O'Neill
Meadow in the Sky —
   A History of Yosemite's Tuolumne Meadows Region

Designed by Mark Shepard and Jon Goodchild,
typeset by Shepard Associates,
and printed and bound by
McNaughton & Gunn, Lithographers.

Yosemite Association
PO Box 545
Yosemite National Park,
California 95389

To the thousands of people
whose lives have been enriched
by walking in the mountains
with Carl.

"Still—in a way—nobody sees a flower really—
it is so small—we haven't time—
and to see takes time, like to have a friend takes time."

Georgia O'Keefe

Contents

Acknowledgements

Writing this book has been something of an adventure, and the best parts of the adventure were the hundreds of hours I spent walking and talking with Carl. He showed unfailing patience in answering questions and in drawing me into the charmed magic circle around him. Most of the interviews were in Tuolumne Meadows, but there were several delightful days at his house in San Jose. He gave me access to his books and papers and to the notebooks written in his youth. It was from the latter that I culled most of the literary quotations at the beginnings of chapters. He faithfully replied to my letters, answering questions about all manner of things. Thanks to Carl.

Carl's daughter and son, Linnea Sharsmith Davis and John Dana Sharsmith, read portions of the manuscript, furnished materials and pictures, and generously and patiently offered comments and suggestions. They both talked with me about their father's life, and they made available to me all of Helen Myers Sharsmith's journals, thus adding immeasurably to the story.

Numberless others of Carl's friends and colleagues, students and admirers, told me stories and cheered me on. Their names are legion so they shall remain nameless, but they know who they are.

Mary Vocelka, as Yosemite Research Librarian and friend, dug out materials and manuscripts and answered questions. I made use of the extensive Sharsmith cassettes in the Yosemite Research Library which had been prepared by Michael Ross and Henry Berrey. Photographers John O'Neill and Milt Irvine contributed photos. My thanks to Shirley Sargent, Ann Matteson, Doris Rubin, and Richard Reitnauer, all of whom read the manuscript at various stages and offered helpful suggestions. Catherine Rose gave precious vacation time to consider it at length and contributed to its clarity, accuracy, and richness of detail. And Yosemite Association President and Editor, Steve Medley, gave his enthusiastic support, kept his cool when I grumbled, and spent many hours and days on the meticulous job of editing.

My husband Carroll shared in the adventure with encouragement, advice, and attention to the many little details that plague and concern a writer. He dredged up his memories of climbing Mount Lyell twice with Carl, shared the walks and evenings with him, and read the manuscript more times than anyone else. I cannot thank him enough.

Carl Sharsmith in a pensive mood. Photo by John O'Neill.

Introduction
Walking with Carl

I t's an unforgettable day. We have left Tioga Pass at the high eastern entrance of Yosemite National Park, crossed a frosty mountain meadow touched by morning sun, and scrambled up a rocky slope beyond the last dwarfed whitebark pine. Now we are on Dana Plateau, a moonscape of broken boulders twelve thousand feet in the sky. We marvel at the pygmy daisies dappling this alpine desert with purple and gold. "Try not to step on them," says Carl.

Big cumulus clouds balloon over the horizon, grow, swell and combine. By lunchtime we are perched on a rocky promontory with several thousand feet of space sheer below us. We can see storms in every direction: west from the Central Valley, north and south above the great Sierran sea of peaks, and east over Mono Lake, a salt-rimmed mirror in the high desert.

The air rings with electricity. When we move, we snap and crackle. Phil poses on a rock cantilevered out over space, and everyone takes his picture with his hair standing eerily straight up.

Carl munches his bread and cheese and then he smokes a pipe. Despite his almost eighty years, he doesn't seem tired. His is the leanness of the mountain pine, a spareness proper to this spare and magnificent world. After a while he suggests mildly that we come away from the edge where there is the most electricity. A kestrel vaults across the face of the storm.

"We're terribly exposed. It isn't safe," someone says. A few chime in, "Let's go down."

But Carl smiles and replies, "It's grand up here. You wouldn't want to miss the storm!" Looking back the way we have come, we know we can never get down to treeline, let alone to the campground, before it hits.

Then the storm is upon us, and Carl leads us to shelter under an enormous balanced boulder. We huddle together swapping stories while lightning flashes, thunder rolls, and angled hailstones as big as fish eyes bounce on the rocks outside. We are all a little bit scared.

"They aren't really hailstones," Carl explains. "They're called graupel, frozen pellets of snow."

When the downpour slackens, a shaft of sun breaks through. Carl shoulders his pack. Without a word, he heads up through the lowering clouds and the still-falling graupel. A few hesitate. "We're cold. Let's turn back."

Carl looks at them, and his face is transfigured. "You know what John Muir would say? 'You can sleep an eternity in your grave. You're only up here a little while.'" He turns and heads up again, and we all follow. The stiff climbing rapidly warms us.

The ground is covered with white several inches deep. Purple daisies, green and gold ivesia and rosy buckwheat are encased in the icy mantle — a white carpet woven with Persian blossoms. The sky is dark and light like an El Greco painting, the rocks are gleaming wet, and we know it is perhaps the most wonderful day we have ever known.

Another cliff edge. We look down more than a thousand feet to Dana Glacier, and the sun comes out to dry us. Carl stares downward. "There's a little sunflower I've found nowhere else in the park but on that black moraine," he is saying, and our minds leap the dizzying space below, sunflowerward.

At the end of the day when we return, Ferdinand Castillo, the park ranger at Tioga Pass, hails us. "We were thinking of you in that storm, but we weren't worried. We knew that Marmot Sharsmith would find a hole to crawl into."

"It was a fine day," says Carl, "the finest I've ever had up there."

Kim speaks for all of us. "Yes, it was! There'll never be another day like it!"

Unless, that is, we go walking again with Carl.

We are members of an alpine botany seminar sponsored by the Yosemite Natural History Association. The seminar began as we sat in a circle on a flowery alpine meadow listening to Carl. Belding's ground squirrels popped up from their holes to watch us, and one rufous hummingbird stopped in midair to inspect a red bandana, then whirred away. Carl spoke slowly, fervently, with a slight smile. He told of the advance and retreat of the glaciers as though they were his children, and of the mountain flowers like a troubadour singing of his lady. We felt, all of us, that we had come not for a college course, but for a pilgrimage.

Later as we picked our way after Carl into a mountain cirque, he hardly suggested a knight errant. When on duty as a ranger, he wears the ranger uniform. But with us he dressed in nondescript khaki pants and a faded shirt. What had once been a tweed jacket settled about his figure like mountain snows fitting the contours of the slope they fall upon. The coat was darned here and there, patched at the elbows, and colored a mottled gray like lichen clothing the rocks themselves. On his back was a not-so-old rucksack given him by a student the year before to replace the one he had darned and patched for twenty years, "after my son tried to throw it away."

Long before Schumacher came up with *Small Is Beautiful*, Carl had perfected his simple, low-impact way of life which suits his frugal Swiss upbringing. To him, old is beautiful; the most striking part of his apparel is his Stetson hat, bought for ten dollars in 1924, which today no self-respecting moth would even consider.

"A fine hat," he says. "They don't make hats like that any more." It still has its jaunty flat brim, but every seam of the crown has been restitched by hand, and the crown restitched to the brim. There is no hat like Sharsmith's hat, monument to a lifetime of wind and sun and storm.

His car is a 1936 Ford roadster. Like the hat, it is well cared for, with more than two hundred thousand miles on the original engine. Carl doesn't overtax it. He keeps it under canvas most of the time and usually accepts rides with other people.

His frugality is legendary — his fifty-year-old flashlight, his diet of beans. But he is never frugal with enthusiasm, kindness, strength or endurance. He gives himself to the mountains and to people like the wildest of spendthrifts. We are all richer for it.

Following Carl, for five days we walk the high places, the alpine fell-fields. We see marmot and pika and the rosy finch that plunges off the peaks and eats insects congealed in snow. Carl shows us a rare saxifrage left over from an icier period, that can only survive deep under shaded rocks with its feet in the cold snow-seep. He shows us which flowers must stand in running water, which can survive only on unstable slopes, and which must espalier themselves to boulders to take advantage of their thin envelopes of warmth in order to grow.

He talks of the grasses that girdle the boreal regions of the globe. He talks of the Coppermine River, the Aleutians, Greenland and Siberia, and they flicker before our eyes until we, too, are walking the tundra in our minds. Our boots sink into the mud as we squint through magnifying glasses at blossoms of sedge and rush and discover strange beauty.

One day he runs his hand through the mosses under the overhanging edge of a tiny meandering stream and comes out with his eyes gleaming and a crumble of earth speckled with blue-green dots. "This is a Siberian liverwort," he announces. "You can always tell it by the peculiar color." What is Carl's magic? We feel that these small dots are a great treasure that has been revealed to us — and so they are. And beyond the grasses and liverworts and saxifrages, loving him as we do, we want to know more about Carl himself.

Too soon the week is ending, and we have our last campfire. When he is ranger for the whole campground, Carl builds a big fire as rangers do. But with us, his little seminar, his happy disciples, he makes his kind of fire: very small. It's warm if we sit close, thrifty of wood, and hardly any trouble to the universe.

Last night some of us had a party in the campground. We ended up a bit tearful because it had been so beautiful and was almost over. This evening the seminar is really over, and we are sobered by the thought. We try to tell Carl what it has meant to us. Even after the tiny fire burns out we linger before saying our goodnights.

Don almost makes a speech. "I've learned a lot, I've met many new species and some higher primates who may become lifelong friends. But the most thrilling experience was being in the aura of Carl Sharsmith. Thanks to all of you for being part of one of the best weeks of my life."

Mary is silent, but I know what she's thinking. This afternoon as we walked back from Slate Creek in the rain, she told me about a dilemma just solved, a commitment newly made. "I've been pulled in one direction and another in my college life," she confessed. "But now I know I want to give my life to botany."

For most of us, though, this has been an interlude, time snatched from our ordinary pursuits to walk in Carl's extraordinary universe. We will go back richer for having made certain small important commitments of our own. We will walk more softly and see more deeply into the nature of things.

Several years and many magic miles after that day on Dana Plateau, I became acquainted with the long story of Carl's life. I have tried to tell his story in the pages that follow. I hope that for those who have known him it will evoke happy memories, and for others it will bring pleasure and a glimpse of a great and memorable and utterly individual Sierran.

Seedling

The Schaarschmidt Family in Salvation Army uniform, London, 1913.

1
Roots & Early Growth

Prussian military power hung over Europe like coal dust in the mid-eighteen hundreds. Some time during that period, because of a distaste for militarism, August Friederich Schaarschmidt left his home in what is now East Germany and moved to Basel, Switzerland. A widower with four children, he became a Swiss citizen, married Salome Langenbach, and fathered six more children. Later he would compare himself to Job: "and there were born unto him seven sons and three daughters."

Schaarschmidt was an architect, and some of the buildings he designed are still standing. Nevertheless, his children grew up in hard times. During the Franco-Prussian war of 1870-71, the older children recalled seeing starving French soldiers trailing the German troops in search of food. The war left in its wake a depressed economy, and with so many young Schaarschmidts there was never quite enough to eat. Between meals, bread was locked away in a cupboard.

One of the family, Karl Wilhelm, pondered a future with little to recommend it and decided to become a baker in order to ensure his future supply of bread. He left school and apprenticed himself to a baker. There followed years of grueling work, getting up in the dark to stumble down and light the ovens at three in the morning so they would be hot when the master baker arrived. At dawn he pushed a small handcart through the snowy streets to deliver piping hot rolls in time for *petit déjeuner.*

Basel was a handsome old city facing Germany to the north and France to the west, a mellow blend of German Protestant and French Catholic culture leavened by ardent Swiss nationalism. Its citizens spoke their own version of *Schwyzer Duutsch* (Swiss German) liberally larded with French expressions, and moved as easily from Swiss to German to French as a housewife moves from room to room.

The city took pride in its elegant red stone cathedral and city hall. On market day the marketplace was filled with farmers from the country bringing shiny oiled cheeses, crisp carrots and cabbages, clucking hens and squealing pigs, and a fragrant variety of sausages to be washed down with hearty Basler beer.

Yet this cultural abundance and grace did not translate into prosperity for the hard-pressed Schaarschmidt family. As Karl (called Charles in the French manner) gradually mastered the skill of producing perfect crusty loaves, he dreamed of America, the land of *unbegrenzte Gelegenheit*, limitless opportunity. Emigration was in the air. An older half-brother departed for the unknown land, and although no word had come back from him, Charles cherished the hope that he would return laden with gold and beckoning for Charles to follow. No word would ever come, and the family could only speculate and grieve. There was yet greater grief to follow. A younger brother found his way to the Alaska gold rush and was murdered. The limitless opportunities were darker and more dangerous than at first imagined.

Meanwhile in 1875, a year later than Charles, Marie Sommer was born in the tiny Swiss village of Tschugg near Neuchatel. Her ancestors had been farmers as far back as anyone could remember, and lived in the Emmental, Swiss cheese capital of the world.

In later years Marie spoke little of her childhood. The Sommers lived on the land, and the land exacted its price in back-breaking labor for young and old. She remembered planting and harvesting potatoes, the whole family in the field together, women in broad straw hats tied on with kerchiefs, men wearing homespun shirts and trousers.

And she remembered the flax: planting it, cutting it, retting it in running water until the green of the leaves was rotted away and only the harsh strong fibers remained. Then beating the flax by the children for hours on end before it could be spun and woven into cloth. Could she ever look at a piece of linen without remembering those days? Yet later her table would always be set on gleaming white store-bought linen, no longer a token of her toil but of the success of her husband.

Most Swiss children worked hard and played little, worshipping with thin-lipped intensity in village churches, and expressing their love of beauty in the fine embroidery of their regional dress, the rich devotional music of their Germanic heritage, and occasional village festivals. Boys like Charles were apprenticed early. Girls, too, had to learn to earn a living, for the land would not support all of a farmer's family. Marie found work as a maid.

About that time a prominent American doctor, physician to President

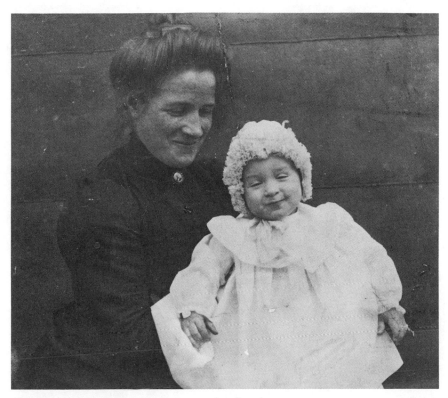

Carl & his mother, 1904.

McKinley, visited Switzerland. During his stay Marie worked for him and his wife. When they finally left for home, the doctor's wife said, "Marie, if you ever get to New York, come see me and I'll help you find work."

Marie treasured that offer, and some time later set out for the new world. She knew only a little English, but had a good measure of gumption and perhaps some desperation to set out alone for so far away, knowing she might never return. In later years she said little about the tremendous adventure of crossing Switzerland and France by railway and boarding a ship full of bewildering crowds of polyglot emigrants. She was young and pretty with blond hair and blue eyes, and she was alone. In New York she made her way to her friend, the doctor's wife, who promptly hired her.

Charles, too, had come to New York as a boy of about fifteen. This was only the first of many times when he would leave a safe haven for the new and untried. After searching for some time he found a job at the Holland House, the finest hotel in New York at the time. At first, although he had a *Lehrzeugnis* or certificate of proficiency as a baker, he did the lowliest jobs, washing dishes and scrubbing floors. Then the chef, Herr Becker, took him under his wing and began to train him. Charles had discovered his natural metier and advanced quickly until in time he became le saucier or saucemaker, second only to the great chef himself.

Charles married an American woman, but the marriage ended in divorce and he was left with a son, August Friederich, known as Gus.

Lonely for home, both Charles and Marie gravitated toward the company of other Swiss, and in time they met and began keeping company. When her employer learned that Marie had a sweetheart, she became concerned, aware of the pitfalls the young blond foreigner might face. Feeling that Marie was her responsibility, and fearful of losing her, she asked, "This young man, does he have a job? What does he do?"

"He works in the kitchen at the Holland House."

"Oh, in that case I'm sure he's all right." The Holland House clinched it.

In 1902 Charles and Marie were married. He was twenty-eight; she, twenty-seven. Marie accepted Gus as her own child. Then on March 14, 1903, she gave birth to Karl Wilhelm the Second, our Carl.

God moves in a mysterious way, and so did Charles Schaarschmidt. He had been fourteen years at the Holland House and was near the peak of success in his chosen calling. Nevertheless, while Carl was still a baby the family returned to Basel.

Back in his home city, Charles opened a bakery at 24 Hagenheimerstrasse. There they stayed for several years — long enough for Carl to remember standing tiptoe by the counter and begging for snippets of dough. These were years of a cheerful active family life with Papa's brothers and sisters, especially *Onkel* Fritz, *Onkel* Hermann, *Onkel* Wilhelm and *Tante* Bertha. Later *Tante* Bertha had a daughter, Gretel, but Carl would not meet her for another sixty years.

Then Charles gave up the bakery and moved the family to London. At first they had hard times there. Father was not well and took to drinking. Marie always had a nice dinner ready for him. But when he came home drunk he went into a fury, pounded on the table, and sometimes even struck her.

Carl, now six and a skinny little towhead, entered a school run by the London County Council on Drummond Crescent. They lived in a flat on

Saint Pancras Street near the railway station, surrounded by high brick walls topped with broken glass, and big iron gates to keep the children in and the world out. Beyond the gates were dreadful slums with drunken women shouting bawdy songs, hawking fish and chips and buckets of foaming beer, and urinating in the gutter — the world of the derelict poor, which he saw first-hand by peeking through the sheltering bars of the gate.

School was also surrounded by brick walls and closed by iron gates. The drinking fountain protruded as an ungainly pipe from a wall, with an iron cup hanging from a chain. Generations of schoolboys had given the cup a swat to hear it ring when they passed, until it had worn a hollow cave in the brick.

Carl's classroom was a not-unpleasant prison where boys chanted lessons aloud in unison, and discipline depended on the teacher's oft-wielded ruler. On Fridays they had stories and special activities. Carl absorbed much of the Old Testament, the Arabian Nights, and tales from English history. There was no science at all, but Mr. Hutton, the teacher, used to exhibit strange objects like a piece of shagreen or sharkskin which struck Carl as marvelous for its rough feel. Each day he looked forward to group singing, for his own home was filled with the high sweet voice of his mother and the wheeze of his father's accordion.

The Titanic was being built in a Belfast shipyard, and Mr. Hutton and his boys followed her progress devotedly until the day of her launching. Shortly afterward came the never-to-be-forgotten horror when the great ship struck an iceberg in the North Atlantic and went down, and over a thousand lives were lost.

Things became better at home. Father joined the Salvation Army and stopped drinking. He was kinder to Mother, and the entire family was happier. Soon Father advanced to become a sergeant major in the Salvation Army, and the family joined what was known as the Deutsches Korps. Every Sunday morning the band marched smartly down the street, Father playing a big bass horn, Mother a bass drum, Gus a cornet, and Carl trailing along behind. They lined up facing one of the foulest public houses for testimonials and songs. Rowdy onlookers usually heckled them, throwing rotten tomatoes and eggs which the Korps endured with stoic bravado.

At an early age Carl understood that middle class people can have no conception of the work the Salvation Army does among the desperate. He also knew that he owed to the Army the now happy home life he enjoyed.

Nature played little part in his life. Yet he showed an early talent for drawing, usually scenery or flowers. He was proud of a daffodil he drew that was hung on the school room wall. Once in a while his parents walked in the park with the children, as Europeans do. And he cherished the memory of an excursion to Brighton: the feel of the sand, a little bucket and shovel, shells, and bright white sails skipping across the water.

When Carl was eight or nine he decided that his name was unwieldy and un-English. His parents agreed that he could anglicize it. A document was signed and filed, and he became Carl Sharsmith.

In 1911 his parents went to Switzerland for a trip and left him with a Swiss acquaintance. He came down with diphtheria and was sent to the hospital to be spoiled by the nurses, and to gradually recover. When his parents returned they were not allowed to visit him in quarantine. At last one day the nurses took him to the window. To his immense joy, he saw both his parents in the street below with Commissioner Railton, right-hand man of General Booth, founder of the Salvation Army. Railton wore a flaming red sweater decorated with a huge gold cross. All three waved happily.

When Carl recovered, he was allowed to visit the nearby British Museum. He was enthralled by the Egyptian exhibit with its dark echoing halls, the rows of smooth sarcophagi, the mysterious benign faces of beast-gods. On the way to the museum he passed the equally exotic scene of the London streets: costers or pushcart vendors who had the curious custom of sewing thousands of brightly colored buttons on their clothes, sooty chimney sweeps, and the huge brewery wagons drawn by Percheron horses, with brawny men in leather aprons rolling the barrels on and off.

In the mornings a boy brought a cart to the door with a tank of milk to fill the housewives' bottles. In the evening came the lamplighter. From an upstairs window Carl could lean out and place a few potatoes or chestnuts to roast on top of the lamp.

His father had found a position in The Charterhouse, an exclusive hotel where he was once more le saucier. It seemed the family would stay in England forever, and Carl would be raised an Englishman. But true prosperity continued to elude them. After seven years in London, Charles had saved only a few hundred dollars.

Suddenly in the winter of 1913 everything changed. They were off to Canada. They dismantled the flat and packed their possessions in willow wicker trunks. Gus, who was in love with an English girl, decided to stay in London. So after saying goodby to Gus, Charles, Marie, and Carl boarded the train for the west coast of England. Passing Birmingham they could see great smelters belching red flames into the night sky as though to celebrate their going, and a cold wind blew. In the harbor at Liverpool was a forest of masts.

The voyage lasted two frigid weeks and was terribly rough. Carl had sometimes thought of being a sailor, but he changed his mind as the ship lurched up and down in the wintry seas. At least he wasn't seasick; his mother credited the prunes she kept feeding him. Father, who never cared much for adventure, spent most of the voyage in his bunk. They were slowed down in a thick fog on the Grand Banks, and as the ship's bell tolled mournfully, Carl thought of the devastating icebergs, and of the Titanic, and felt the deep awful fear of the sea.

The steerage was packed with European peasants, mostly Russians headed for Canadian wheatfields, the women in full thick skirts and colorful kerchiefs, the men in bushy beards. When the ship tied up in Halifax, they lined up with Carl's family to go through customs.

At St. Johns, New Brunswick, the ship was sheathed with white frost from the Newfoundland fogs. On a chill February day in 1913, Mama's willow wicker trunk was lowered to the pier in a big net, and Carl stepped ashore in the new world where he had been born. He was ten years old.

Snow was piled in arctic chaos along the streets, and tall black crosses lined the snowy roads — telephone poles, which Carl had never seen before. As they proceeded toward their lodgings, a small man swathed in heavy clothing approached. He had a swoop of drooping mustache that ended in amber icicles stained by chewing tobacco. Oh, brave new world that has such people in it!

They took the train to Montreal and were soon settled into a flat. Father got a job as chef on the Imperial Limited, the crack Canadian Pacific train, and was gone for two weeks at a time on the Montreal-Vancouver run. He took great pride in his position, recounting how roomy the kitchen, how fine the service, how superb the food. Yet he often spoke longingly of the balmy climate of Vancouver at the other end of the line.

Carl was entranced by the city in its wintry splendor, the continual ringing of sleighbells, and the muffled thud of horses' hooves on hard-packed snow. He began to go to the great central square after school. It was a clanging bustling place with no obvious traffic rules, and dozens of spirited horses drawing sleighs with curved prows and long runners extending out behind. The other boys caught rides on the runners, and Carl soon learned the trick of it.

Once he discovered that he had boarded a junk-sleigh piled high with bottles and sacks. The red-faced driver was urging the horses on at a breakneck pace. When he turned back and saw Carl, he roared, "Get off me sleigh, damn you!" Terrified, the boy clung tighter and watched transfixed as the man snatched up a bottle and hurled it at his head. Letting go at the last moment, Carl skidded onto the street, with horses and sleighs streaking by in every direction. Somehow he recovered his footing and made his way home, too shaken to confess.

After the first excitement, the winter seemed to drag. The sparkling snow grew dingy. The cold was wearisome, requiring an array of caps, scarves, mittens, and long underwear constantly smelling of wet wool. Father continued to talk about Vancouver. "There we can live without all this dirty snow," he announced.

Carl felt a little afraid of his father, yet Charles had his gentle side. Sometimes he took his son by the hand and led him down to the train station. What glorious, powerful monsters the engines were! Carl climbed into the cab and talked to the engineer, and felt that he, too, could drive this harnessed giant.

In spring his mother took him to visit a house where she worked, and they went into the long garden to see some towering elm trees. Running to touch the trunks, he pulled his hand back in disgust. "What's that sticky stuff?" he asked, staring at his gummy fingers.

The grownups laughed, and his mother explained, "That's to keep caterpillars from climbing up and eating the leaves." He gazed at the froth of green shade above and thought what a shame it would be if they were all eaten up. He never learned to love caterpillars, but he was beginning to know the magic of trees.

That summer they finally did move to Vancouver. The train ride across Canada with his mother was exciting — the hustle and bustle of many people, luggage to manage, meals in the dining car where the water in the glasses barely jiggled as they glided along. Prairie grasses waved like green tides, and enormous cumulus clouds rolled over the sky, stately as schooners in the wind.

Passing through what were called colonists' cars, he saw the Russian immigrants again, sitting on wooden benches along the walls with their babies and satchels, and hope in their eyes. Now and then the train stopped amid jerks and blasts, unknown portentous noises, at a cluster of buildings that seemed to have been dropped onto the imperturbable gigantic sea of grass. A few people got off or on. Sometimes there was a mysterious wait before a shattering clank announced that this place was about to disappear into prairie again as though it had never existed. For the boy with his nose pressed to the window, Canada seemed to go on forever, tranquil, enormous, and strange.

Then the prairie began to heave and swell into hills and finally into mountains. Dark sentinel lines of trees appeared, banks of glittering snow hung high and suspenseful among the rocks, and the railway banks were bright with flowers. Outside of Revelstoke, British Columbia, the train stopped for a long wait. The mountains rise steeply above this small town by the young Columbia River, but Carl hardly noticed them. He dashed out to feel the meadow turf under his feet and, in an ecstatic rush, to pick the flowers. As he gathered an armful of blue and red and yellow blossoms he lost all sense of time, and came back to the person-world only when he heard his mother's frantic call, and the train pawing the track and chuffing like an impatient stallion. He climbed aboard just in time, so rich in flowers he hardly heard his mother's gentle scolding.

Vancouver was a busy port full of boats and buildings. Afterwards what Carl recalled most was walking with his mother along a railroad trestle to Stanley Park. There his breath was almost taken away by the soaring douglas firs losing their tops in a soft gray mist from the sea. Among these mysterious presences, ravens spread their black wings and croaked mournfully and wonderfully as though trying to tell him something.

The douglas firs set their seal on him. In some secret, inviolable core, Carl now belonged to the trees.

Within six months after the move to Vancouver, the family crossed yet another border, and eleven-year-old Carl (first American, then Swiss, then British, then Canadian) came back to the land of his birth to stay. They now settled in Portland, Oregon. Papa and Mama bought a restaurant named The Bismarck half a block from the Morrison Street Bridge, and Uncles Fritz and Hermann came to live with them and work in the restaurant. These uncles would remain significant figures in Carl's life.

Uncle Fritz was intelligent and observant, with bright penetrating eyes, close-cropped hair, and a little mustache. He always wore dark serge suits with immaculately clean linen shirts. At this time he was a widower with two daughters, and he never remarried. He was a master patissier or pastry cook, and turned out the most elegant and mouth-watering confections.

Uncle Hermann had a Roman nose, the same little mustache as Uncle Fritz, and a lifelong scowl. His face always seemed to say, "Everything is going to pot right now." He worked as a cook, but never reached the culinary heights of Charles and Uncle Fritz.

Both brothers were ardent socialists and liked to engage Charles in terrific arguments. Their hero was Eugene V. Debs, and they looked forward with glee to the demise of the capitalist system. Charles, on the other hand, was more conservative and an outspoken patriot. He was tremendously proud of his American citizenship, which he had received shortly before Carl's birth, and frowned on his brothers' politics. Nevertheless, the three were to remain close the rest of their lives, exchanging long letters and visiting when they could.

For a time Fritz's daughter Nellie stayed with Carl's family, but frugal old-worldly Marie disapproved of Nellie because she wanted to dress in the latest style. "Latest style! What's that?" demanded Marie indignantly.

The Willamette River was a busy place, and Carl was thrilled by the tall masts and the huge rafts of floating logs — those same douglas firs he had come to love, now limbed and topped and smelling like pickles as they drifted downstream to the lumber mills. The air was soft, the sky delicate blue or gray, and both rain and sunshine were gentle.

The Schaarschmidts lived in a house on Fourteenth Street with a huge Royal Anne cherry growing next door. Its branches hung over into their yard and gave them a sweet harvest of fruit. The street was lined with handsome chestnut trees that in autumn dropped brown nuts to roast. Their fragrance brought to mind the smoky portable stoves of the London chestnut vendors in October.

Carl went to Ladd School. That year the Liberty Bell from Philadelphia was on tour around the country. Carl's teacher took the class to see the bell, and they all solemnly kissed it.

Marie was known even among her penny-pinching Swiss relatives for her frugality, and she never indulged in the extravagance of buying toys. Yet Carl yearned for roller skates, as all the other children had them. Somehow he obtained a single skate and skated so hard with it that his pushing shoe began to wear out. His mother finally concluded it was cheaper to buy him a pair of skates than to lose the money in shoe leather.

The Willamette was not the Mississippi, and Carl was not Huck Finn, but he had many an adventure in this river town. Soon he had a little gang of friends. They called themselves the Black Handers, and devised a secret logo crowned with the skull and crossbones. They wandered widely in the immensely diverting city. Sometimes they pulled a handcart down to the docks and collected slabs of douglas fir bark dropped by the stevedores as they loaded the ships. This bounty they sold for firewood at five cents a cartload.

One day as they passed along the street, a large balloon loomed in the sky ahead, surrounded by a crowd. Worming his way to the center, Carl saw a man in the basket calling, "Ballast, we need more ballast. Who wants a ride?"

He waved his arm frantically. "Me, sir, take me!"

"Well," said the man, "here's a fine young fellow for ballast. Come aboard." He leaned over and pulled him into the basket. By standing tiptoe Carl could look over the rim at the crowd, who cheered wildly. Then the ropes were loosened, all except one to keep it from floating away altogether. The balloon began to rise, and Carl's excitement with it. Soon they were above the buildings and he could see that the city was on a broad plain. Above the blue-green countryside, the snow-capped Cascades rose like apparitions: Mounts Hood, Jefferson, Saint Helens, Adams, and even the crown of distant Rainier. He spat over the rim, noting to himself that this was his longest spit.

"It wasn't so scary," he told his big-eyed pals when at last he returned to terra firma. They were impressed.

The gang often went to the woods, especially to a hill they called the Butte. There under the dappled shade of maples and alders and douglas firs, they acted out their fantasies of being wild Indians or explorers. Marie made a cloth case for a whiskey bottle so Carl could have a canteen. One day the bottle fell out of its case and broke, spilling milk on the ground to hoots of derision from the tough Black Handers.

A Swiss dairyman named Mr. Cadenau delivered milk daily to The Bismarck. When summer came, eleven year old Carl was sent to live with the Cadenaus on their farm near Hillsdale about seven miles from the city. He cherished the countryside: green pasture surrounded by ragged douglas firs, and a bountiful kitchen garden full of delicious vegetables. He smelled the sweetness of berry bushes, fruit trees, and meadow flowers, talked to the cows and birds, and warmed toward a girl named Viola with blue eyes and an impish smile.

The day began at four in the morning when Heine, the son, milked the two dozen cows and turned them out to pasture. Then the milk was cooled and the cream separated in a huge metal vat about three feet high. Carl could lean over and drink out of this lake of milk with his lips. Breakfast was served about six, then the milk was poured into fifteen-gallon cans, loaded into the wagon, and Queen the horse was hitched up to take it to town. Later Grandmother Cadenau churned the cream in an old-fashioned churn.

In late afternoon the children went to the far pasture and called the cows, who started walking majestically toward the barn with their calves. Carl loved stroking their downy noses and gazing into their big brown eyes. After getting to know them, he watched with horror when a kosher butcher came to the farm. According to Jewish dietary laws he methodically slit the calves' throats and the blood gushed out in a red stream.

Evenings they sat in the parlor, fancy with antimacassars and family daguerreotypes, a Bible with gilt edges, and a player piano playing the popular song, "Oh, Honey Boy, I hate to see you leave me."

At harvest time the farm hands came, and the several Cadenau women labored in the kitchen until noon, when they set a long table laden with bountiful and delicious food. The family and many of the hands chattered together in Swiss, but the children always answered in English. The Cadenaus assumed their children would be fully assimilated into American culture, and made little effort to preserve their Swiss identity.

The summer with the Cadenaus was an idyllic interlude. When Carl went home in September the First World War had begun, and his world had changed. Suddenly anything that was or even seemed to be German was bad. It did not matter that Mama and Papa were Swiss; they too suffered from discrimination. And their restaurant had an all-too-German name.

Things had not been going too well with the restaurant, anyway. Charles was a perfectionist. Everything had to be made with the finest ingredients by the most meticulous methods. Carl used to love to go there, stuffing himself on home-made doughnuts and fried razor clams. But his parents seemed unable to charge as much as their labor merited, and they ended up in the red.

So they gave up the restaurant, their last venture into business by themselves. In 1915 they said goodby to Portland, to the Butte and the bridge, the house and the cherry tree, and looked for a new home in Salt Lake City.

Salt Lake is far from the big douglas firs, the green meadows and soft misty skies of Portland. Yet it has its own splendor — burning sunlight throwing everything into glaring contrast, and lavender mountains standing in sharp detail against a brilliant sky. The sun went down like a ball of fire, and afterwards the mountains flamed red and purple before the light went out.

The city was laid out in a grid of great wide streets where it was impossible to get lost. Soon Carl was wandering by himself. He was exhilarated by the clear mountain air and the cool sound of water flowing from handsome bronze fountains and running in a perpetual stream along the gutters. It seemed like a new Eden.

Charles was chef at the Newhouse Hotel. He had become clean-shaven not long before, but when he reported for work at the hotel, the manager was outraged. "When we hired you in Portland, you had a mustache and beard," he said. "If you want this position, you'll have to grow them back." Even in those days, image was king. For the rest of his life, Charles always wore a mustache and a neat little goatee.

One day in Carl's school, the teacher told the class, "Run to the window and look out." They heard a roar overhead and glimpsed the first airplane any of them had ever seen.

As in Oregon, the boy followed his bent to seek out nature wherever he lived. In his rambles into the country he discovered City Creek Canyon, where on weekends he spent long days alone exploring. His mother made him a knapsack for these expeditions.

He yearned to know the names of the plants — the ones that love dry sand, those that seek out seeps of water, and those that hug cliffs or burrow against dry rocks. But he had to content himself with a nodding acquaintance and no proper introduction. No one could tell him their names. If a plant wasn't edible or otherwise useful, it was some sort of weed, and that was that.

Salt Lake City was only a mirage in time, for soon they were on the move again. What demon drove Carl's father time and again to desert a safe berth for the unknown? Why had he left each position, even crossing the Atlantic in midwinter, as a wanderer — a man who didn't even enjoy travel? Any answer would be only guesswork. The pattern continued down the years until Charles reached the lotus land of Southern California, and there he stayed. Meanwhile, Carl's childhood was a kaleidoscope of locations. He formed no real attachments anywhere. Only with time would Carl fashion his own sense of place, and set down deep and enduring roots in California's High Sierra.

2
Galveston on the Gulf

"Affable live-oak, leaning low, —
Thus — with your favor — soft, with a reverent hand,
(Not lightly touching your person, Lord of the land!)
Bending your beauty aside, with a step I stand
On the firm-packed sand,
*   Free*
By a world of marsh that borders a world of sea."
—Sidney Lanier

Late in 1915 the Schaarschmidt family left the spacious desert for the hot muggy Texas coast, where Charles became chef at the Galvez Hotel in Galveston. They stayed until early 1919. In this formative period of early adolescence Carl's mind began to stretch and grow.

Galveston occupies a low sandbank on the Gulf of Mexico. They arrived just as the people were recovering from a fierce hurricane. Almost destroyed by a previous hurricane in 1914, the city had built enormous ramparts which this time saved it.

The entire country was astir with the First World War. On the streets of Galveston, the newcomers saw cranks brandish wooden guns at unemployed men, and occasionally they felt anti-German sentiment. One day at school the teacher was questioning the class about milking cows. For Carl this was familiar ground, and he gave her the correct answers in the only words he knew for milking — Swiss-German. She snapped, "Incorrect," gave him a bad mark, and remarked on his rosy cheeks, a vaguely foreign trait where all the other boys were sallow.

How different Galveston was from any of their previous homes! The land was perfectly flat, and Carl missed the mountains. All the buildings were made of pitchy yellow pine which burns with tremendous heat. Shortly after their arrival a nearby hotel burned to the ground, and the next day Carl wandered among the smoking ruins looking for treasures.

The family moved into a little house near the beach with a large Madeira vine growing over it, a castor-bean tree in the back yard, and lots of warblers. The house was so small that Carl had to sleep on a screened-in porch. For the first and last time they took in a boarder, the maestro of the Galvez dining room orchestra. This European gentleman arrived with a big brown setter named Fritz, who every day had to have a prime rib of beef medium rare, obtained from the hotel.

Carl began to be more aware of his father as a chef, and of the peculiar constraints his occupation laid upon the family. Charles worked in the mornings and came home each afternoon about two. While he took his nap, all had to be quiet. If flies woke him with their buzzing, he roared until someone came and drove them away. If Carl made a noise, Mama scolded him. After the nap, Papa went back to work and stayed until late in the evening — to Carl's secret relief, for now he could better enjoy his mother's company and pursue his own interests. Yet his father had a congenial side too, and often regaled the family by singing songs of the Gay Nineties. "The Bowery" was one of his favorites.

Papa and the maestro ate at the hotel most of the time. When Charles arrived he was served by the *commi* or messenger boy at a special table. He could have ordered anything in the house, but he ate very simply, usually just soup and salad, and never grew fat like the typical chef.

Galveston's resort area at the beach had bathhouses, dance halls, and an amusement pier. Though the pier could have held endless fascination for an adolescent boy, Carl seldom went there and had little interest in the gewgaws he couldn't buy anyway. In his home the existence of this rather sinful, or at least suspect, sector was never mentioned, though at night they could hear dance bands playing the airs of the day. He did go to the bathing beach, and once in a while his mother came with her friends. Marie seemed to find women friends wherever she lived; almost invariably they were Swiss. They wore the bathing suits of the time with bonnets, skirts, long stockings, and shoes. A little splashing was what they called a swim.

Carl began to hang around with skinny-necked Charlie McGinnis and lean, hard Harold Duble who had a Texas drawl and a shotgun. One day as they were roaming the countryside, Carl spotted a rabbit. On an impulse he seized Harold's gun and fired. The recoil nearly knocked him down, and the rabbit was blown to bits. He felt sick and ashamed, and never again tried to shoot a living creature.

Harold was captain of the baseball team, and soon Carl was playing left
field on the corner lot. When banana boats came in from Central America,
the boys picked up bananas that were dropped in unloading and sold them
for loose change. In warm weather they went swimming and fishing, roamed
the sand dunes, and waded into the sloughs feeling with their toes for oysters
which they ate right out of the shell. Carl began to find beauty among the
rocks and shells on the long sandspit. The only trees were tamarisks, called
salt-cedar, and there were myriads of birds.

At school Carl's teacher, Miss Brock, a rather plain woman with a soft low
voice, told the class about Odysseus and the fall of Troy and other incredible
stories and legends. She read them poems by Lanier, Bryant, and Longfellow,
and Carl's heart was stirred.

He was lucky with Miss Brock, for other classrooms were out of control.
He thought the other students were nothing but wharf rats. On the play-
ground they fought and swore, called him a damnyankee, and cornered him
and gave him a bloody nose every chance they got. He learned to defend
himself, but the constant fighting was alien to his nature.

By the age of fourteen, he had had enough. He quit school. This was not
unusual in those days, and no one protested. Charles knew he could train
Carl in his own profession, which he never doubted was the highest and finest
that any man could follow. Though he was perturbed by Carl's evident lack of
a true calling to the kitchen, perhaps it was not too late. He put the boy to
work with him at twenty-five dollars a month. Carl never saw the money for it
all went to his mother, financial manager of the family. Nor did he question
his new role. It was simply what he had to do, and he did it.

In its own way, the kitchen was a wonderful place. Charles anglicized the
written menu but continued producing a rich continental cuisine. He was in
his element bustling importantly among the intricate preparations for a fancy
banquet. Once during a big convention, he and the headwaiter began sipping
the wines too liberally. (Charles was no longer a teetotaler, but Carl had never
seen him overindulge.) When, whooping and hollering, he picked up a pan
and beat out a tune with an iron spoon, Carl slunk into a corner in humilia-
tion. "Oh, Papa, how could you?" he thought.

As Charles had fondly hoped, the boy began to learn. Soon he was making
whipped cream eclairs, petits fours, and macaroons of pure almond paste. He
created Napoleons of puff paste turned seven times to form thin flaky layers,
filled with pastry cream, covered with white icing and crossed by curved lines
of melted chocolate. It was, as his father so firmly believed, a noble craft —

and for a growing boy, great eating.

There were some tasks less pleasant, like the preliminaries to making green turtle soup. The animal was brought in alive, laid on its back on the butcher's block, and teased until it put out its head. The cook forced a sharpening steel into its mouth, drew the head out further, and cut it off. Charles thought this barbaric process was only a slightly disagreeable step in making a most agreeable product, *potage de tortue*. Carl was revolted.

Carl's busy life was leavened and enriched by two great joys: books and nature. He had always been a good student and an avid reader. After he had devoured what he could in the children's room of Galveston's Rosenberg Library, he moved into the adult section. What riches he found! Although he loved poetry and stories, he was quickly drawn to natural history. In his rambles he was looking more and more closely at the trees and rocks, birds and flowers about him. And in the library he discovered that they all had names, genealogies, histories, and their place in the world.

He came across Ernest Thompson Seton's writings and began to study woodcraft. Seton showed him how to make hickory bows for himself and his friends. Then he read Hough's *American Woods* from cover to cover, admiring the alternate pages with specimens of wood cut in fine sheaths. He would, he vowed, learn the trees. He would find more than salt-cedar and beach scrub; he would find trees like those he remembered from Oregon, from Vancouver, and even like those in the idyllic paintings of John Constable, the great oaks and elms of far-away England.

Another landmark book for Carl was Ridgway's *Birds of North & Middle America*. Although the print was small and hard to read, and birds were identified by such obscure features as hairs in the mouth that could be seen only with the dead bird in hand, it nevertheless opened a new world to him.

There was so much information and wisdom that Carl wanted to master. Yet somehow in his family one never bought a book, and he didn't feel he could do so. He started a series of notebooks, creating his own private library. The notebooks exist to this day, small and worn and full of treasures. In them Carl kept an intermittent journal of his trips afield, adorned with drawings and sometimes cast in the form of romantic stories in which he and his friends figured as Indian braves. He carefully transcribed a wealth of information and quotations from his reading.

In October, 1916 he began "Camp Cooking, Recipes, wrote by Carl Sharsmith." There followed instructions for making campfire bread, beans, etc., copied from Seton and others.

Early in 1917 he started the "Tally Book of a Woodcraft Indian, Rover Band" with seven pages of Indian symbols and blazes, signs made by bending and breaking twigs or grass, by piling stones, and even by smoke signals.

In March he recounted an all-day campout with the boys. "We started at 7 o'clock and Harold couldn't get his shoes on, but got them on at last. It was pretty cold and thin ice covered the little ponds. When we got to English Bayou the sun rose. We followed the trash pile trail and waded through ice cold water. Halfway to Skeleton Camp (Harold calls it Skelekon Camp) we found the bones of the dead cow that we seen last hike...In the middle of the bones was a big pile of manure which probably was the cause of its death...Harold starts the fire with 1 match while Bennett rustles firewood and I rustle breakfast...pretty good breakfast...Harold climbs up the big cedar trees around Skeleton Cave. We discover a good lookout then we start trimming off the small branches...after a while we practiced throwing the tomahawk at a piece of board (and find out that we're bum shots)...Bennett keeps on saying, "Aint it dinner time yet?" I rustle dinner and we have Boiled rice with bacon gravy and fried bacon, pretty good...I find a pretty straight piece of cedar and start whittling on it and start making a little bow and use my shoestrings for a bowstring. We start shooting with it but it's too weak. Bennett grabs it and starts shooting at some buffaloes till we have to take it and throw it away...Dinner time...I rustle dough for Hot bread and bake it in Harolds soldier frying pan and fried bacon and raw onions. (pretty good dinner.)...On the way home we passed by the ponds that were frozen over in the morning and find hundreds of little mullets (frozen to death?) along the banks. I forgot to say that a big flock of seagulls were swimming on Synor's bayou probably for the dead fish. About half past five we arrive home in safety."

For Carl these expeditions were filled with wonder and excitement. Sometimes he wrote in the third person. "The two braves had just arrived at the sand dunes when they heard a sound, and sinking down in the tall weeds they watched...Suddenly two white men with rifles appeared and the keen eyes of the red men who lay hidden took in everything...they glided through the vegetation of the dank forest. A song sparrow sang unsuspicious of their presence as these superb wild men glided through the thickets of the mosquito jungle." As they threaded their way back along the bayous, the sunset sky was filled with hundreds and hundreds of ducks. It seemed to him he was not on a sandspit in Galveston; he was a noble redskin in a pristine wilderness.

Galvez Hotel. Photo courtesy of the Rosenberg Library, Galveston, Texas.

In February, 1918, he designed a decorated title page to "Notebook, Little Beaver of the Band of White Buffaloes." Throughout 1918 his attention was riveted on birds. He found a dead sandpiper on the beach and drew its head. He compared the beaks and feet of different species. When market-hunters brought ducks to the hotel Carl drew the feathers in loving detail and stored them in a box. He also made extensive bird lists, accompanied by careful drawings labeled with indications of color. By this time he had been drawing for years and excelled in accurate representation. It's a masterful set of sketches, all done on small pages in pencil; they suggest the early work of a future Roger Tory Peterson.

He found a book on the plant kingdom. Sitting in the kitchen at the Galvez and waiting for requisitions from the storeroom, he began illustrating the different orders from mosses to ferns and up to the flowering plants.

These are only a sample of the riches in Carl's notebooks. He painstakingly copied the woodcraft sections of the *Boy Scout Handbook* with tent patterns, rules for hygiene, and more camp cookery. There are animal tracks and star constellations, lists of foods consumed by different species of birds, diagrams and description of how to measure the height of a tree, scraps of poetry and aphorisms by famous people, and sketches of trees, camps, and, later, of mountains. Beside his drawing of a plover he remarked, "Coming home from

sand hill camp found this bird clinging on sea wall soaking wet. I climbed
down and put him in a dryer place. When I set him down he cried like a little
chick. I hope he comes out all right." On April 29, 1918 he sketched a
swamp with an ovenbird and a rose-breasted grosbeak "identified absolutely."
In May of that year a flight of frigate birds crossed the top of the page.
"These birds are the most wonderful fliers I have ever seen."

His mother often talked about the Swiss Alps, and from an early age Carl
had yearned for and idealized the beauty of the mountains. Now in his library
explorations he began to learn about American mountains. And the dearest
books of all, the books that would illuminate his entire life so that henceforth
it glowed with an inner warmth and purpose, were those by John Muir: *The
Thousand Mile Walk to the Gulf, My First Summer in the Sierra, The
Mountains of California, Our National Parks.*

Sitting on his little screened-in porch under a bare bulb on summer nights
while mothwings whirred about the light, Carl lost himself in Muir's magic
words. In the distance a band was playing "Smiles", and the romantic music
blended with the romantic writings and stirred him deeply. He could see in
his mind the tall sequoias and the glow of sunrise on the peaks, the sugar
pines, the rippling streams, the glaciers, and chills went up and down his
spine.

In his notebooks Carl patiently wrote out long sections by Muir and read
them over until they were imprinted in his memory. Thus Muir went with
him the rest of his life, whispering in his ear and his heart the summons to the
wild world, the mystery and beauty of creation. He saw nature, the nature he
had always turned toward, in a new way — as Wordsworth said, "appareled in
celestial light."

Now he would venture forth alone like John Muir into the wilderness. An
electric train crossed the causeway connecting Galveston to Houston, and
beyond the causeway were the woods. One Sunday Carl took the train and
penetrated this region of oaks dripping with Spanish moss, tall grasses, and
companies of birds. There were no streams, but many pools inhabited by
great garfish with mysterious long snouts. To Carl they seemed like prehistoric armored creatures. About him was a vibrant, ringing peace.

He decided another time to stay overnight in this wonderland. His mother
had made him a knapsack and a ticking to fill with leaves and Spanish moss
for a bed. After a vast flaming sunset he settled under the majestic oaks and lit
a little fire. He had brought some sandwiches, and as he munched and shiv-
ered a little, he listened to bird calls and strange croakings. He imagined that

he had cut himself off from civilization and its discontents and found The Way.

In the night he felt a horrible itching all over. He relit the fire and checked himself but could find nothing, so he lay back down to scratch and toss until daylight. When dawn finally came he packed up, still itching, and hungry because he had eaten all his supplies, and headed for the road. Beyond, he saw a field. He wriggled under the fence and made a breakfast of freshly-filched sunwarmed watermelon and fresh-dug peanuts. Back on the road, he headed toward the causeway to catch the train.

A black man driving a wagon stopped and picked him up. As they jogged along he turned to Carl. "What you doin', white boy?"

Carl shrugged casually. "Just lookin' around."

"What you scratchin' for?"

Carl fell into the language. "I itches, I does."

"Chile," said the man, "I knows what you gots. You gots de chiggers. You get your mamma to wash you down wid kerosene, dat'll fix 'em."

So the years of Carl's adolescence were passing, with forays into literature and into the woods, and dutiful days of fetching and carrying, cooking and snacking on caviar and filet mignon in the kitchen. His father had a fine position, but he was again dissatisfied. A new manager had arrived with the idea of efficiency. Now the chef had to account for everything — no more free-and-easy with the supplies, the special perquisite which Charles considered his due. He felt constrained and insulted and began casting around for another job.

He had two attractive offers, one in Knoxville, Tennessee and one in San Francisco. He and Marie discussed the choice at length but couldn't make up their minds. At this point, as he would many times later in life, Papa came to Carl. "What do you think, Carl? Which should it be?"

Carl didn't have to think twice. His eyes glittered in anticipation. "Take California!"

Sapling

3
Home to California

"Going to the mountains is going home."
—John Muir

In February, 1919 the Schaarschmidts boarded the Southern Pacific train for California. Sensing a kind of homecoming, fifteen-year-old Carl was wildly excited. California was the land of Muir and of Muir's mountains, and he belonged where Muir belonged. "Goodby, Southern Yellow Pine and Sunny South. Westward Ho!" he wrote.

As the train chugged westward, Carl slept in the upper berth above his parents. He woke at two in the morning determined to get up and see the mountains. But when he started to climb down, Papa yelled, "Get back to sleep!" He lay still and waited until he heard his father's even snoring, then rose again and slipped past him. Snatching up the big overcoat that was Charles's pride and joy, he hurried out on the platform of the observation car.

The train was sliding across the desert like a noisy rattlesnake. Carl watched transfixed as sunrise turned the looming mountains from blue to purple, then red to gold. His notebok, adorned with hasty sketches of desert plants, reflects his elation: "This will be a day to remember...it was my first day in the mountains, but it will not be my last...Now I can truly believe John Muir when he says 'The Mountains of God.'"

As the train whirled along, Carl failed to notice that blowing dust had turned the overcoat a dingy gray. He returned to his parents bubbling with excitement, but his father was furious at the state of his coat. Mama, ever the peace-maker, shook out and brushed the coat, and harmony was restored.

Coming into the San Bernardinos, Carl saw deodar trees for the first time and was entranced by these imports from the Himalayas with dark swooping boughs and lofty tops.

Arriving in Los Angeles (announced by an electric sign: GREATER LOS ANGELES, 250,000 POPULATION BY 1925), the family had some time to spend before continuing to San Francisco. Carl heard there was a railroad up a nearby mountain, and he persuaded his parents to take the excursion to Mount Lowe.

At the end of the line it was snowing, and Papa, never fond of outings and especially not in a snowstorm, was in a blue funk. A fire roared in the Mount Lowe Tavern fireplace, and Papa and Mama sat down shivering and holding out their hands to the warm blaze. But Carl ran outside and raced up through the chaparral, exhilarated by the mountain air and the swirling snow.

"I did not follow the trails, they were too tame for me," he confided to his journal, "so I went straight up a certain canyon and looked for the wildest place possible and found in a hollow beneath a massive strata-like rock covered with lichens and mosses, some beautiful delicate ferns. Here I rested for a spell, eating some bread I happened to have, and the while feasting my eyes on the beautiful views about me. I then returned the way I came, scrambling and sliding down the steep slopes, four times as fast as I traveled going up and soon arrived at the Alpine Tavern. Found my parents ready to return but I was loath to leave such a wonderful place, but bowed to the inevitable."

In San Francisco they moved into a flat with a bay window, and Papa worked in the Saint Francis Hotel as *saucier* under Chef Victor, his idol. The kitchen was a babel of French commands: *"un poulet, écrevisses, huitres!"* Carl was taken on as *garde manger*. This meant that when the cook shouted for supplies, Carl brought them up from the storeroom. He also beat eggs and olive oil into a thick creamy mass to produce fifteen gallons of mayonnaise at a time, and made ice cream flavored by vanilla beans with a heady intoxicating fragrance.

The Schaarschmidts, father and son, worked ten hours a day, six days a week. The routine was trying, and Carl yearned for a different life. "Beautiful day but plenty of work. Had to put on a new suit and shoes which I can barely tolerate. I really wish I was a savage."

On Sundays he took long walks, and soon discovered Golden Gate Park and his first *Sequoiadendron gigantea*. "Noble tree! If I live long enough I will yet see King Sequoia in all its primeval majesty! Excelsior!" He fell into the habit of walking the entire length of the park, reveling in exotic trees and flowers, and then out to the beach and dunes, windswept and washed by a wild cold surf so unlike the almost-tropical waters of Galveston Bay.

One day Carl had walked long and far and grew very hungry. Immersed in books as he was, he began to fantasize. He had been rereading John Muir's *Thousand Mile Walk to the Gulf*, and recalled how Muir bought some bread when he was almost out of money. He was, Muir wrote, on a jubilant march through Georgia eating his beauty bread. Beauty bread — that was it! When you are hungry, bread is beautiful. Feeling akin to Muir, Carl found a bakery and bought a bun, the little incident rich in associations. Much of his experience in life was to be of this kind: a humble detail, but touched with poetry and hallowed. In later years he shared this feeling of romance with those who walked with him.

On his sixteenth birthday he climbed Mount Tamalpais. "Saw one rabbit and a lot of noisy jays near the summit and I wished I could be one of them."

On March 25th he visited Muir Woods, a grove of coast redwoods, for the first time. Along the way grew maidenhair ferns. "Many are the times I have dreamed of you and tried to write poems of you!" he exclaimed. "But here you were at last, making all the forest and rocks glad and Lovable. Long may you Florish!" He approached the sequoias reverently. "I ran here and there to this tree and that, examining and talking to them in a hushed voice," he wrote.

Carl returned to Muir Woods many times, fascinated by the vegetation, the views, and even the other people. On the ferry ride to Sausalito, many young people were singing and playing ukeleles. On Sundays, the narrow-gauge Mount Tamalpais train (self-advertised as "the crookedest railway in the world") took him from Sausalito to Muir Woods, where dozens of people got off and spread out picnic lunches. Carl quickly learned that when the whistle signaled departure time, the picknickers left everything and hastily climbed aboard. He regularly feasted on abandoned pieces of cake and pie.

Heartened by his success in living off the country, he decided to sleep out under the soaring trees. He found a secluded little gully to crawl into, wrapped himself in his red and blue striped blanket, and slept a holy night in a cathedral of redwoods.

Now that he was in his own view a man of the trees, he devoured the works of Horace Kephart, dean of woodcrafters, though he wondered at the thought of bread raised by the yeasts in lichens and baked in a bucket, and puzzled as to how to get boughs for a bed from the majestic California trees. On the title page of Kephart's *Woodcraft*, bought in March, 1919, he copied from Byron's "Childe Harolde":

"To sit on rocks, to muse o'er flood and fell,
To slowly trace the forest's shady scene;
Where things that own not man's dominion dwell
And foot of man hath ne'er or rarely been.

To climb the mountains all unseen
With the wild flock that never needs a fold;
Alone o'er foaming falls to lean.
This, this is not solitude; 'tis but to hold
Converse with Nature's charms
And view her stores unrolled."

Inspired by Kephart, he searched for edible plants in the field, and noted, "Found an herb which I thought must be Solomon's Seal, I dug up the 'long bumpy storehouse of food,' washed it and tried to eat it, but it was tough and unpalatable and gave me a burning taste in my throat all day. Probably it is not good till cooked and it might have been the wrong plant."

He was also mastering the skills of backpacking. For Carl, backpacking had the aura of Indian life as filtered through the rosy spectacles of the romantic literature of his day. To be a noble redskin, he thought, was the next best thing to being a carefree animal of the forest.

One of his favorite books was George Washington Sears's *Woodcraft*, published in 1884 under the Indian pseudonym of Nessmuk. Nessmuk was a little 110 pounder as tough as nails. He lived in the Adirondack backwoods for long periods and came to know intimately the Indians and their ways. Sixty years later Carl could recite much of his book verbatim:

"The coming gloom warns you that night is shutting down. You are no tenderfoot...There is plenty of small timber standing around...Five minutes suffices to drop one of these, cut a twelve foot pole from it, sharpen the pole at each end, jam one end into the ground and the other into the rough bark of a scraggy hemlock, and there is your ridge pole. Now go...for the bushiest and most promising young hemlocks within reach. Drop them and draw them to camp rapidly.

"Next, you need a fire. (After preparing kindling and shavings) strike a match on the balloon part of your trousers. If you are a woodsman you will strike but one. When you have a blaze ten feet high...tackle the old hemlock, take off every dry limb, and then peel the bark and bring it into camp...Next, shingle (the young hemlocks) on your ridge pole. This will make a sort of bear den...Before turning in you make a cup of tea, broil a slice of pork, and indulge in a lunch....You are warm, dry, and well fed.. .It is two bells in the morning watch when you awaken with a sense of chill and darkness. The fire has burned low and snow is falling...You rouse the fire, and...get out the little pipe, and reduce a bit of navy plug to its lowest denomination...again you lie

In the kitchen, Mount Diablo Country Club, 1920. Marie and Carl stand at left, Charles is second from right.

down — to again awaken...to find the fire burned low, and daylight breaking. You have slept better than you would in your own room at home. You have slept in an Indian camp."

Backpacking gave Carl freedom to wander farther afield. On one memorable occasion, he walked over fifteen miles from Mount Tamalpais to Bolinas and camped in the trees on a high ridge. Not having a camera, he documented his camp by drawing it. On this hike his eyes were drawn to the grasses, and he observed, "Am now anxious to see the flower in every grass and grain I find."

He did not yet suspect that botany would be his life work. Musing before the fire in the apartment at Laguna Street, he wrote, "John Muir's writings, I believe, will help me decide the course I shall take in life." He added with Swiss severity, "Perseverance wins!"

In the spring of 1919 Carl's family left San Francisco and moved to the Mount Diablo Country Club near the foot of Mount Diablo. They lived in one of the small wooden houses provided for employees along a creek. The California countryside was green and gracious, the valley oaks delicately twisted and filling with new leaves as the season progressed. By late May buckeyes along the canyons of the Coast Range burst forth with huge pyramidal clusters of creamy bloom, and the fragrant air was full of bird song.

Papa was chef of the country club, Mama worked in the kitchen, Uncle Fritz made the pastries, and Carl produced pies, muffins, and ice cream, turning the freezer by hand. It was a happy family time. Papa's job was to equip the kitchen, and he insisted on all copper pots. Many decades later Carl visited the club with Shirley Sargent, Yosemite historian, and found his father's copper pots still hanging above the stove.

On his one day off a week, Carl often climbed Mount Diablo. An old wagon road led part way up, but he never met anyone on it. This flowery mountain top and the vast expanse of valleys and hills were his alone. When the sky was crystalline clear he could see the High Sierra, a distant tantalizing promise of glistening snows.

From his climbs of Tamalpais and Diablo, he made a chart to rate the two mountains in terms of beauty, vegetation, trails, and view. Mount Tamalpais won by a nose.

When he climbed Tamalpais, he usually returned to San Francisco and caught the train for Walnut Creek. One night he reached Walnut Creek very late, ten miles from home and no way to get there but on foot. He tried to thumb a ride, but no one would stop. On he walked through the fragrant darkness. As he approached an old farmhouse in Danville, some dogs began to bark. An upstairs window was thrown open and the owner stuck out his head. "You get the hell out of here," he roared, and slammed the window shut.

So Carl went down by the creek and slept under the sycamores until dawn, when he gathered up his gear and hustled home.

All the while, Carl was learning the flowers. He had bought a second-hand copy of *The Foundations of Botany* by Bergen for ninety cents. As he educated himself, he used the book as a guide to make drawings and take careful notes. He was on his own, dogged and solitary, and a little bit odd because he set so much store by flowers in a world where life was real and earnest, and pastries more important than potentillas.

4
The Big Woods

"Out of this wood, do not desire to go.
Thou shalt remain here, whether
thou wilt or no."
— Shakespeare, Midsummer Night's Dream

Before long, Carl realized it would be possible to work in the forests he loved so much, to actually earn money going where he longed to go. Two ways seemed open to him: lumbering and mining. He chose lumbering. The hiring halls, popularly called the "Slave Market," were on Howard Street in San Francisco. Outside them, big blackboards listed the number of muckers, teamsters, timber fallers, and other workers needed. A man stated what he could do, paid a dollar, and was issued a train ticket and directions to a work camp.

In September, 1919, at the age of sixteen, Carl went down to the "Slave Market" and got a job in the big woods.

He took note of the bedrolls, called bindles, the loggers carried, and assembled one for himself: two "sugans"*, a toothbrush, and some extra clothes in a homemade pack. He was now a "blanket stiff" or "bindle stiff," a member of the higher echelon of lower society.

At the bottom of the heap were the bums who wouldn't work, but begged or swindled the companies for petty cash or goods. On his first trip Carl saw bums pay a dollar, get the railway ticket, then hop off at Shasta Springs before reaching the job. When a man arrived in camp, he could be fitted out with new clothes at the company store and have the cost deducted from his first pay check. Some bums went so far as to check in, pick up the clothes, and skip. The worst of all were what they called "whiskey stakes"—

---

*sugan: an old Scotch-Irish term brought to the Appalachians by early settlers, and spread by their descendants among cowboys and lumberjacks to the west coast; often a patchwork blanket made of old clothes and stuffed with cotton batting; in Carl's day, a cotton quilt.

Logging train in Shasta National Forest. Photo courtesy of Ray Kite.

men who worked until they had ten dollars and then disappeared into skid row on a drunken spree, not to emerge again until they were down and out and sober. (Carl was never to see liquor in the camps proper.)

The typical bindle stiff wore fifty-cent jeans, eighteen-dollar logger's boots, a forty-five-dollar Hamilton railway watch, and a ten-dollar Stetson hat. Remarkably, the prices remained stable for fifty or sixty years. Carl wore jeans but no watch, and shoes at five dollars a pair. A Stetson would come later, in other circumstances.

He signed on as a swamper to clear brush and smaller logs from the forest floor so the horses could come in and drag out the big logs. At the McCloud Camp near the town of Sisson (now Shasta City), he found himself in miles and miles of mature Jeffrey pines with sweet-smelling cinnamon-colored bark and autumn winds singing in their long brushy needles. The twenty-five loggers lived in small bunkhouses furnished with iron cots, wooden boxes, and kerosene lamps.

In those days there were a plethora of jobs and a shortage of workers, and no camp could hold its men unless it fed them well. All the camps had pigpens for kitchen slops, and served a lot of pork, along with stews and soups, pies and cakes, piles of eggs and mountains of pancakes. Even to a palate adjusted to caviar and oysters, the food seemed great. But then, it was served up with the sauce of ravenous appetites from hard work.

Carl started at three dollars a day and later worked up to four and a half. He paid a dollar a day for board. With no place to go and nothing to buy, the money piled up quickly.

He was doing hard physical labor and loved it. Ten hours a day (in addition to the time going to and from the job) left him glowing from head to toe with health and enthusiasm. He grew strong and skilled in handling an axe, easily wresting tough manzanita root-crowns from the soil and lopping off limbs the size of a man's arm with one clean cut.

Sanitary facilities in the camps were nonexistent — not even pit toilets, and no laundries. Nevertheless, clothes had to be washed, and that was the first task every Sunday morning. The men dumped their shirts and long underwear into a rectangular five-gallon oil can full of soapy water, and agitated them with a plunger made of a can full of holes fixed to a stick.

Sometimes on a Sunday afternoon Carl walked alone in the forest. It was a keen delight after long noisy hours of work to go quietly, to listen to nature, and to contemplate the straight round boles of the pines. The trees inspired him, but in order to be close to them he was forced to take part in their slaughter. At least the ruthlessness of logging was mitigated. Instead of clear-cutting, the loggers carefully left behind the new growth or "reproduction" to make a new forest. Even the horses were trained to walk around saplings without trampling them.

One of the favorite pastimes in camp was smoking. All the men had pipes; they called cigarettes "coffin nails." Many of them had worked in the Michigan woods and used Peerless Tobacco, a two-fisted favorite of that region.

One day a boy about Carl's age arrived in camp to work as a water boy. He swaggered into the bunkhouse wearing a big black ten-gallon hat.

"Where are you from?" Carl asked.

"My home is where I hang my hat." He peered around anxiously and pulled out a big pipe. "Y'got any whiskey?"

"I don't drink."

"Y'got any tabacky?"

"I don't smoke."

The boy reared back and let out a snort. "Ain't you got no comforts nohow?"

One snowy day not long afterwards, the men were all in another cabin playing cards. Alone in the bunkhouse with nothing else to do, Carl picked up a pipe and lit it. It was the beginning of a lifetime of devotion.

Another day the timber fallers cut down a bee tree. The honey, gallons of it, was way back inside and must have been very old for it had a dark greenish color. In the spirit of the old woodcrafter Nessmuk, Carl scooped out a bucketful and took it to the cookhouse, where he hung it in a cheesecloth bag by the stove. It dripped slowly into the bucket below and gave him thick sweet honey — until the morning he found a dead mouse in the pail.

After some time as a swamper, Carl was promoted to toggle-knocker. When the horses dragged in logs on wagons with ten-foot wheels, it was his job to knock the toggle or catch on the bull chain between the wheels to release the logs. If he hadn't timed it just right he would have been crushed by the descending logs. With boyish optimism, he never thought to be afraid.

He worked through the fall of 1919. By Christmas, winter had closed in and the camp shut down. Carl could have gone back to the kitchen with his father, but wrote, "I could never probably work indoors again." Instead, he found a job in the coast redwoods with the Goodyear Lumber Company at Elk, south of Mendocino City.

In contrast to the vigorous cheerful life at McCloud, the Elk Camp was mean and dirty. At McCloud most of the men were old-time woodsmen; here Carl encountered a polyglot mixture of novices from all over the world with little experience and no common culture. Nobody could understand anyone else's lingo. They lived in measly bunkhouses with two bunks jammed into each, so full of fleas and bedbugs that the men placed small cans of kerosene under each leg of their iron cots to keep the bugs away. There was no refrigeration so the meat was smelly, and even the chimneys of the coal oil lamps were never cleaned. Instead of a fine lunch brought out to the crews, they filled their pails with leftovers stacked on the end of the breakfast table. They went to work before dawn and came home after dark.

Carl never got into the standing redwoods. He was fireman on the donkey engine, sawing and splitting wood to fill the fire box. The donkey, a small auxiliary engine that hoisted the logs as they arrived, was very old and about ready to blow up. All he could see were redwood logs coming down and bark peelers prying off the spongy fibrous red bark. The buckers sawed high, wasting vast quantities of wood, instead of fifteen inches from the ground, as the Forest Service rules had required at McCloud.

For the first time in his life, Carl became homesick. Before a month was out he threw in the sponge and headed for San Francisco. He noted, "Heartily disgusted...Came home again...find I love mother, etc., more than ever."

5
Jim

*"Those friends thou hast,
and their adoption tried,
Grapple them to thy
soul with hoops of steel."*
— William Shakespeare, Hamlet

After a brief stay at home, Carl was itching to get back to the woods. In February, 1921, almost eighteen, he decided to try his luck at Sacramento's "Slave Market." He arrived late in the day and had to stay over. Never one to spend a dollar unnecessarily, he walked around with his bindle in the gathering dusk until he came upon the capitol building surrounded by tall dark redwoods. Creeping under one of them, he spread out his bed and slept the night.

The next morning he surveyed the job market. Employers were drumming up work on the O'Shaughnessy Dam in Yosemite's Hetch Hetchy Valley. They had posted big signs: "Work on the Hoochy-Koochy! Good pay, good food, and ice cream for Christmas!" Carl, steeped in John Muir's writings and his opposition to the dam, wasn't tempted.

He signed for a job on the Caribou Project of the Great Western Power Company. Boarding the ferry for Oakland, he stood by the rail staring across the water at a flashing advertisement for Heinz 57 Varieties, as the men behind him passed a bottle and wondered why he didn't take a slug. In Oakland the workmen caught the train for Belden on the North Fork of the Feather River. The first night they slept among boulders by the river, shivering in their thin cotton sugans, and the next morning climbed up to the camp on the side wall of the canyon.

The camp was run by the Stone and Webster Company, building a tunnel for Great Western's penstock. The cabins stood on stilts strung along the side of the canyon and were connected by a boardwalk. Each morning the silence was broken by the sound of Mike O'Donohue, the camp boss, coming down the boardwalk in his hobnail boots bawling, "All oot, all oot! R-r-roll oot or r-r-roll up!"

Carl was detailed to the bull gang for roustabout work. That meant general labor: moving heavy loads, emptying freight cars, and carrying ponderous rails that took four men to lift. He was happy on the gang. He particularly enjoyed going uphill in the early morning to the blacksmith's forge to warm the boxes of dynamite by the fire.

One day after working a full ten-hour shift, the men were sent out for an entire night fighting a forest fire. Coming in exhausted to breakfast, Carl tucked away thirteen eggs and then started in on the pancakes. It seemed like a great life.

However, some days later strawboss Tommy Tully sent him to the kitchen. The dishwasher had got his ten dollar whiskey stake and taken off, so Carl was set to washing dishes. The cook told him to empty the leftover mush down a hole in the wall, but the trapdoor to it stuck. He went outside and crawled under the cookshack to see what was wrong. A vast mess of frozen glop slanted downhill from the trapdoor like a glacier. With a pick from the tool shop he chopped his way up the icy slope to clear it — his first ice climb.

On one of his rambles he climbed down to the half-frozen roaring river. There he noticed a little bird perched on a frozen stob and singing away above an opening in the ice. To his astonishment, the bird suddenly dived through the opening into the swirly slush. While he was wondering if it was possible for birds to commit suicide, it emerged, realighted, and took up its singing again. Some time later he realized that this was the water ouzel about which Muir had written one of his most charming essays.

Carl felt he had truly arrived in the mountains. He made a drawing of the woods and labeled it, "I am now in the great Sierran forest." To learn the trees, he made a habit of going up the slope after dinner to study the differences between ponderosa and sugar pine, incense cedar and white and douglas fir. They could be distinguished tactually as well as visually, he discovered. After dark he would test himself by feeling the bark and needles, then write a note naming the tree. The following day he returned and checked his findings.

In the evenings the men sat and talked while the younger fellows whittled shavings to start the stove in the morning. Carl was mesmerized by what he heard. Their swearing was short on four-letter obscenities and long on intricate baroque references to Satan, his grandmother, his mother-in-law, and so on down the generations. They swapped yarns about horses, the quality of

the grub in the next camp, or how someone got a dirty deal — no Paul
Bunyan tales, lttle politics, and never a word about religion.

One evening they got to talking about trees. A man sitting in a shadowy
corner spoke up. "You boys think you seen trees, but you haven't. I seen
them. Twelve feet, fourteen feet, eighteen feet through!"

"Ah, what you talking about?"

"Yes," the voice went on, "I have seen these trees and I am tellling you the
truth. They are big. In 'fifteen I helped build a bridge across the Tuolumne
River at the Soda Springs in Yosemite, and I had a chance to go visit these big
trees. I got down there and ah, they were grand! But one thing I didn't like.
They had puny tin signs on them saying General Tucker, General Smyth, stuff
like that. Well, I reached up and pulled a sign off and stuck it down behind
me. Then I pulled another off, and another, and hid them all under a log.
Then I sat down to enjoy the trees."

There was a long pause. "I've got to know that man," thought Carl.

In this way Big Jim Wyllie, bull cook and roustabout, entered his life. He
was a huge braw Scot past fifty with squint eyes, big nose, caulifower ears,
lantern jaw, bull neck, and hands like pine knots. He had been a sailor in the
declining days of the clipper ships, a sourdough in the Alaska goldrush, and a
Canadian doughboy in France in the First World War.

Jim filled Carl's ears with tales of far-off New Zealand, its Rotorua Geysers
and its strange "vegetable caterpillar" with vines growing out of its head.
(Later Carl learned that the "vines" are a parasitic fungus.) He told about the
men called kauri diggers who search under the exotic kauri trees for a gum
that drips on the ground, and was valued for use in varnishes.

He spoke of the great ports of the world (he seemed to know them all),
and of the clipper ship, the most marvelous device for using natural energy
ever made by man. Sailors on the clippers had different chanteys for every
kind of job. Jim bemoaned the fact that so little was remembered of the ships
and chanteys, and hoped to write a book about them one day.

In fact, Jim loved books, especially poetry. In his Scots brogue he
declaimed much of Byron's "Childe Harold's Pilgrimage" and the works of
the Canadian poet Henry Drummond, as well as passages from Shakespeare.
He and Carl learned new poems together, sharing Sidney Lanier, and Carl
introduced him to John Muir. It was pure joy to Carl to talk about things
close to his heart with a sympathetic listener. "But Car-r-rl," protested Jim,
rolling the r's, "you ought to develop your own writing style. Don't ape John
Muir-r-r so much."

Jim was a socialist of the old school and ranted against the injustices he had seen and the "capitalist bastar-r-rds" who were the cause of it. He kept telling Carl to "spend your money while it's at par-r-r," apparently expecting an imminent collapse of the economy. His predictions were only a decade off.

Absolutely forthright and honest, Jim always corrected Carl when he made mistakes. Carl, fond of grandiose pronouncements, once said, "Money is the root of all evil!"

"No, Car-r-rl," Jim replied, "It is love of money that is the root of all evil."

Washing his face after work, Carl announced, "Cleanliness is godliness."

"No, Car-r-rl," explained Jim patiently, "Cleanliness is next to godliness."

When Jim noticed Carl's fascination with nature he said, "I'll tell you what. I have this friend named Ansel Hall. We were in France togither in 'sixteen in the Forestry Division of the AEF furnishing timbers for the trenches. He does some kind of nature work in Yosemite National Park. I'll write and tell him about you, and maybe he'll give you a job."

"Oh, don't do that, Jim," Carl answered. "I like this job just fine." What he really meant was that he felt too shy to pursue it. With Jim's help and a little bit of luck, he might have come to Yosemite many years sooner than he did. But fate had more threads for him to unwind until that day.

Some time that winter Carl took off for a visit home. From there he climbed Mount San Antonio in a blinding blizzard that covered all the trees with silver icicles.

Back on the job, there had been a strike on the main railroad line and supplies ran short. Then the flatcars brought everything at once: kegs of railroad spikes, ties, rails, and switches. The men were already working hard ten-hour days, and now they were told they had to go out after dinner and work until midnight. There was some grumbling but all turned out.

Carl was exhausted and unwell at the time and he asked the boss, "Do you mind if I don't come out tonight?"

"If you don't, you get your time in the morning."

Resigned, he went back to his bunk after dinner to lie down a bit and fell into a deep sleep. When he woke the next morning and reported for work, sure enough they sent him to the time keeper, who paid him off and fired him.

Terribly dejected, he hunched over in his bunk and tried to think what to do next. He was a woodsman out of work. Jim came in. "Why Car-r-rl, what's the matter?"

On hearing Carl's story, Jim was indignant. "They can't do that to you!"

he exploded. "The next time I'm in San Francisco I'll report this to the labor commission, and they'll fix it up. Those Goddamn corporation-lackey bastar-r-rds!" He thought for a minute. "Listen, you come over to the cookshack in an hour and I'll have a swag for you."

When Carl had rolled up his bindle and reported to the cookshack, Jim gave him some bacon, potatoes, and onions in a can with a wire bail. "Now, you go up to Camp Two, and if they won't take you, go on to Camp Three. And let me know what happens."

Carl started up the trail. When he topped the hill he found himself in an upland covered by a virgin forest of majestic sugar pines rising over two hundred feet above him. It was early spring and although the ground was still snowy, hermit thrushes were singing. His heart was happy.

In the crevices of an enormous burned-out pine he found a white sparkling crust: sugar pine sugar. He gathered about a cupful in his bandana, then wandered on until he saw Camp Two at the lower end of Butt Valley.

He had his swag, so why not declare a holiday for a few days? Alongside the meadow stood a huge douglas fir with a snow-free space where he spread his sugans and made camp. Sweet fresh water ran in the nearby creek, and there was plenty of wood for a cozy fire. For three days he lived under the douglas fir roasting potatoes, listening to the wind in the trees, and curled up snugly at night. It was more romantic than his first Galveston campout, and no chiggers!

On the third day the weather turned stormy, and while he was getting water from the creek a coal popped from his campfire and burned a hole in his sugan. He was about out of potatoes anyway, so he rolled up his gear and headed toward the camp.

Soon he came to a sawmill with a narrow-gauge railroad to serve it. As he stood uncertainly on a platform by a shed, around the bend came a handcar carrying a crew and the inevitable Irish strawboss. Taking in Carl's outfit at a glance, the Irishman bellowed, "You want a job, Slim?"

"Sure."

"Jump on, then."

Now Carl was a railroad man. The cookhouse in Camp Two was an old two-story village hotel, and the men lived in army tents. Each tent had a Sibley stove shaped like a teepee, with an inverted cone to hold the fire and some gravel beneath. They could see the flame, yet the smoke went up the chimney.

At first the crew just ran up and down in the handcar checking the tracks.

Then a snowstorm hit. Carl had to stand above the cowcatcher on the front of a locomotive staring forward into the blinding storm and signaling to the engineer what lay ahead.

The first day he went out to lay track, someone advised him to carry some spikes "because you never know when they might come in handy." He appeared with his pockets bulging with heavy ironware and got the horse laugh. When the next green member of the crew did likewise, he joined in the laughter.

In repairing track, the foreman sighted along the rail to see where it sagged. Then one of the hands got out the big jack and lifted the rail so that the ties could be tamped. They had to gauge the right amount of slant around curves, and sometimes turned and bent the rail. It was quite an art.

There were other skills. It was wonderful watching a man drive a railroad spike with a maul-head the size of a quarter, gradually drawing the spike very accurately toward the rails. They never seemed to miss. And in drilling holes in the tracks, one man held the drill and two others hammered while he gave the drill a little turn with each blow, perfectly fearless, confident his partners knew their job.

Carl was shortly promoted to gandy dancer. He stood opposite another man, the two alternately shoveling gravel under the tie in rhythm. They had to swing lively and keep in step. One of Carl's tamping partners beat the time by singing a single line over and over, "All the way from Pike. All the way from Pike."

Prohibition was in force, but now and then foreman Pat Murphy took a snort of "blood tonic" out of a bottle, rubbed his belly, and passed the tonic around. Carl let it pass.

Four men could pick up a handcar and lift it on and off the rails. One morning Murphy, who loved to show he was boss, gave the order to take the handcar off. "Put it on again." They did. "Now take it off." After repeating this four times he grinned. "Thanks, boys. I just did that to show me author-r-rity."

Occasionally Carl went to visit Jim Wyllie in the old camp. He had to walk along a half-rotten wooden flume full of running water and ice, strung along the side of a sheer cliff wall. As he groped through the dark, he realized how perilous it was.

"Ain't you got a lantern?" asked Jim. "I'll fix you a bug." He cut a hole in the side of a tin can, fastened on a wire bail, and set a candle inside.

Jim tired of working at Camp One and came up to be with Carl and work for Pat Murphy. But Jim had no reverence for Murphy's authority. One section of track had been laid across a frozen meadow, and now it began to soften. Eventually an engine coming along the track sagged into the soggy meadow. The men stared fascinated as the locomotive slowly sank in mud up to the wheeldrivers. Jim had only scorn for such planning.

The men began to quit and drift away and finally only Jim was left on Murphy's crew. As Jim worked, Pat walked up and down. Finally in exasperation Jim said, "Mr. Mur-r-rphy, haven't you anything else to do but watch me work?"

"Of course not. I'm the boss."

"Well," said Jim, "you needn't bother to come out this afternoon because I won't be here." And he quit. Carl loyally followed.

They walked the road toward Westwood in Lassen County and took a job with the Red River Lumber Company, a division of Weyerhauser. They didn't like it. They got no money, just coupons on the company store, and had a particularly obnoxious little strawboss pacing back and forth and glaring at them if they stopped for a smoke. Finally Jim handed the foreman the axe. "Here, do it yourself!" That was the end of another job.

Carl had been saving his big heavy silver dollars in the bib pocket of his overalls, wrapped and fastened with a horse-blanket pin. "Now, Car-r-rl," said Jim as they headed out, "you get down to town and put that in the bank." In the first community they came to, they stopped outside a bank.

"Go on, go in," said Jim, and Carl obeyed. The bank floor was tile, and in his heavy logger's boots with steel calks in the soles, he slipped and fell flat on his face. The clerks giggled. Angry and embarrassed, he walked up to the first teller and began to struggle with the blanket pin. At this the clerks laughed aloud. Meanwhile Jim was peering through the window and gesturing to urge him on. After a tremendous effort Carl extracted the money from his pocket, opened an account, and rejoined Jim. Deep down underneath he has never liked banks much since.

Escaped from the bank, Carl and Jim left town and walked along a dusty country road. They hadn't gone far when a Model T Ford passed them in a great cloud of dust. Jim lost his temper and sat down on a log to pull out his bandana. "Damn the dust! And damn this Califor-r-rnia sun, it hur-r-rts my eyes," he growled.

The dust had no sooner settled than along limped a little dog, apparently dropped off by the Model T. Now Jim was madder than ever. "Those sons of per-r-rdition!" He looked at the dog. "You poor little fellow, you've got sore feet. We'll fix some mocassins for you." He tore up his bandana and made booties for the dog, and off they all went down the road.

As they were skirting Lake Almanor strange dogs came out and barked at them. "I'll find a place where they won't plague us," said Jim. They went on until they discovered the lonely Prattville cemetery where they rolled out their sugans and slept, undisturbed by the many ghosts named Pratt who inhabited it.

Walking on the next day, they came through groves of tall spreading sugar pines and felt they were in a great cathedral. Jim reverently removed his hat.

When they parted in late spring, Jim kept Carl's address, and afterwards they corresponded. Jim's letters were always written on the margin of a magazine page or a scrap of newspaper in a fine Victorian hand, and were full of pithy observations.

They didn't meet again for more than a decade. In 1932 when Carl was ready to enter graduate school, he decided to look Jim up in British Columbia. He bought a steerage passage on the Dollar Steamship Lines from Oakland to Vancouver. It was a miserable trip. Carl and his fellow passengers ate under a greasy winch dripping oil onto their food from the deck above. The ship rolled in high seas, and the foul air in steerage made everyone queasy.

"Hey, fellows," shouted one of the boys, "the bosun's left the bulkhead open. Let's go up in first class and get some fresh air!" Soon Carl and his new friends were sitting in deck chairs wrapped in steamer robes and sipping tea brought by obsequious stewards. It lasted until they saw the bosun, a hulk of a Swede, looming over them. He grabbed them two at a time by the scruff of the neck and shoved them below deck. "You get back down there and stay!" he roared, slammed the bulkhead shut, and locked it.

Carl had written that he was coming, and Jim met him at the dock. They took a ferry across an inlet, then a bus, and finally walked a mile or so to Jim's little cabin in the deep woods. He was living on a Canadian military pension of about thirty dollars a month. His homemade stove was of sheet iron with pieces of tin for stove lids. He could only survive by buying almost nothing, his only luxuries a small phonograph and some books. But he was terribly proud, and although he had Scottish neighbors who would have been glad to help him, he indignantly refused any assistance. He prized independence more than anything on earth.

Though poor in goods, Jim was rich in friends thereabouts. One was the curator of the Vancouver Museum, a Scot like himself. Another served as both captain and crew on an ugly old coal boat. A third was an officer of the Canadian Pacific Railway liner "Empress of Ireland," and came to call in a spanking clean uniform with gold epaulets. Carl, Jim, and the officer went down to visit the coal boat, which had been hauling coal from Nanaimo to Vancouver.

The captain emerged from the hold all grimy and took them stomping over the coal to the captain's cabin on the poop deck. To Carl's surprise it was immaculate, even elegant, lined with polished birdseye maple. "This, my boy, is the hull of a real clipper ship," Jim told him. "It's more seaworthy than the Empress out yonder." Its officer agreed.

"Now you walk up and down this hull," Jim continued. "If you see a straight line anywhere, let me know." No chance of that; it was curved in every dimension. Carl wondered why the masts were set back at such a sharp angle. "That's the rake of the masts," Jim explained. "She'll ghost along through the water with barely a wind."

Jim was in his element on board ship where he knew far more than Carl. Back on shore, it seemed at first just like the old days when they had been the closest of friends, and Carl had looked up to Jim as a source of wisdom. They walked in the magnificent forests of virgin fir and talked as they had long ago in the woods. But time had rushed on, and both of them grew uncomfortable. Carl now had the pride of a college education, and Jim felt it. As they conversed in the cabin or walked through the woods, if Carl dropped the name of a plant, or a writer, or mentioned a new idea, Jim mumbled, "He's puttin' on airs," or "that damn professor stuff!" His strong character had rigidified, and he scored Carl out for dumping washwater on the ground. "You put that down this hole," he cried. "It'll never dry there till Kingdom Come!"

On the last morning, instead of his usual oatmeal Jim mixed a big bowl of batter and began to fry pancakes one at a time in his tiny skillet. Slowly he accumulated a big stack. It occurred to Carl that the ones on the bottom were cooling and the ones on the top were hot, and he picked up the pile and turned it over. Jim flew into a rage and went stomping out of the cabin.

Carl thought he'd soon be back, and calmly continued frying the cakes. But Jim did not return. Soon Carl would have to take his bus. He went outside and called, but there was no answer. At the last possible moment he picked up his knapsack and left, closing the door behind him with a heavy heart.

About a year later he received an envelope in Jim's Victorian handwriting. He felt a flood of warm feelings as he held it in his hand. Inside was only a small pressed twinflower, *Linnaea borealis* from the northern woods. Jim had forgiven him.

Although Carl kept Jim's letters for years, somehow he lost track of him. He would always remember, though, his days with Big Jim Wyllie, one of the best friends he ever had.

6
Mount Shasta

"Manual labor is a great good but only in its first proportion. It must be joined with higher means of improvement or it degrades instead of exalting."
— William Ellery Channing

The summer of 1920 found Carl back in the Jeffrey pines, this time at Weed, northwest of Mount Shasta. It was great to be in the woods again. He felt in his bones that the indoor perfectionism of a chef's life could not keep him from the trees.

At first he worked as a limber, clearing felled logs of their branches. A buckboard wagon came out at lunch time carrying huge pots of stew and racks of pies. Long hours of axe-swinging made the food disappear at a fearful rate. After filling up on stew, Carl would eat half a pie at almost one gulp.

A faller named Charlie Whitted needed a falling partner, and Carl heard the men discussing it. "How about Sid?" (Carl's nickname of the moment. Sometimes he was Slim.)

"Aye, I think he'll do," came the answer. So Carl went to work with Charlie, a great woodsman about fifty years old who became a fast friend. The work was hard and called for skill; a slip could mean disaster. He was now raised to the sumptuous sum of five and a half dollars a day, and felt rich and proud.

There were two other timber fallers he particularly admired, Kentucky Slim and Oregon Slim, both about seven feet tall. When 'Kentuck' was falling (woodsmen never said 'felling') he talked all the time. "Down in Tennessee we have yeller poplars dern near as big as these here pine." He meant tulip trees, *Liriodendron tulipifera*.

The two Slims worked together, vying to perfect their craft. Once toward the end of the day they lined up a series of pines all cut partway through so they would fall against each other. When the whistle blew, the Slims falled the last tree, and down they went one by one like dominoes, boom! boom! boom! lined up toward the landing in a perfect row.

On July 4th, 1920, Carl decided to climb Mount Shasta. From the camp at six thousand feet it was an eight thousand foot climb — a major undertaking for one day. Alone, he doggedly pushed up through Jeffrey pine, fir, and finally whitebark pine into the great slagheap of volcanic rock and sand. Although the weather was hot below, it grew cold as he went higher. On the steep upper slopes, he slid back almost as often as he inched forward. He crossed long snowbanks hardened by freezing night temperatures, but softening in the strong summer sun. With his army shoes he was able to kick steps, but the slick leather soles were tricky to manage. Mountain climbers used hobnails, but Carl had none.

At last he pulled himself over the last hump of rock and snow and stood on the top — like Alexander Selkirk, monarch of all he surveyed. This, his first high peak, would always seem to Carl to have been his greatest, most liberating climb. He already considered himself a woodsman; now through this single exploit he had entered the company of mountaineers.

On the way down the mountain he contoured to the north to see the Whitney Glacier, and commemorated it in a drawing he would keep forever. However, his leather-soled shoes betrayed him. He slipped and half-fell, half-slid for what seemed an eternity before he was able to thrash and claw to a halt and avoid disaster.

Unused, too, to the fierce mountain sun, Carl was terribly sunburned. The next day they put him to work on the log-jammer, and all day long he toiled with the thick gritty volcanic dust painfully irritating his burned skin.

Charlie Whitted had a little stump ranch near the mountain. When Carl told him about his climb, Charlie said, "Maybe from the top I can see my forty acres of brush on a side hill." So on September 5th, with nothing but a Hershey bar between them, Carl made a second ascent of Shasta with Charlie.

On the way up, as they were taking a rest Charlie pointed to nearby Goose Mountain. "They're building a fire tower up there, the Forest Service is. But it's a mistake, Carl, my boy."

"Why a mistake?"

"You'll see, Carl. One day there'll be a big walloping fire instead of these here little piddly ones that blow up roundabouts. They'll be sorry they didn't let the little ones burn out all that loose brush. You'll see."

Charlie was right. Carl was to live to see the forest and park services setting controlled burns to get rid of accumulated undergrowth and thus prevent major fires. It's called fire ecology now, but this old woodsman would have laughed at the fancy word and called it common sense.

Mount Shasta rising above McCloud, California. Photo courtesy of Ray Kite.

How many lessons Carl learned from Charlie! At the end of each workday Charlie took the saw to the saw filer, and every morning he picked up a newly filed saw so sharp it could cut out shavings like noodles. When they were working, the saw always gummed up with pitch. They'd stick a tuft of pine needles into a bottle of kerosene, trim it off straight, and make a sprinkling bottle to cut the pitch.

When they were falling a tree, they used the axe as a plumb line to figure how much the tree leaned. They left one inch uncut for every foot of lean. The uncut inches served as a hinge to swing the tree around to the desired direction of fall. Very rarely they would hang up a tree in another tree's branches. When this happened they'd start falling the second tree, carefully twisting it around to take them both down together.

In Weed, Carl learned even more thoroughly the lessons of hard work. In one non-stop stint of twenty-four working days without a single day off, he earned the tremendous sum of two hundred sixty dollars.

Life in the camp had its grimness and tragedies. There were no medical facilities, and, of course, no workmen's compensation. Ed, one of the teamsters, was driving one of the big wheels when the hub of the axle struck a slender lodgepole pine. The top of the tree slewed off and fractured his skull. He made it back to the bunkhouse where Carl tried to stanch the profuse bleeding, while the time keeper got sick at the sight of the blood. They carried Ed to the sawmill for help, but he died. Carl felt heavy with sorrow. This death seemed so harsh, so wrought by blind chance, and Ed was so helpless and alone.

One day not long after that, Carl and Charlie were at work. At quitting time the men ran to the landing where the logs were being loaded, in order to ride back on a flatcar. But Charlie grabbed Carl's arm and said, "No, let's walk this time." They reached camp before the train did, and were just sitting down to dinner when they heard a thin, eerie, far-off locomotive whistle. They knew something had happened. Oregon Slim grabbed an axe and Carl followed him. As Slim strode right over three-foot-high fallen logs, Carl hurried around them toward the unknown catastrophe.

The logs had been loaded onto all the flat cars except the one just behind the tender of the locomotive. The men jumped on this empty flat. The tracks were laid in soft volcanic ash, and as the train picked up speed the tracks came loose. Approaching a curve, the train had begun to sway with the momentum and finally toppled onto the slope below. The loaded cars had crushed forward toward the engine, squeezing together like an accordion the flat car on which the men sat.

When Carl came on the scene it was a nightmare of blood and broken bodies. Eighteen men were killed outright, and the rest crippled for life. There was nothing to do but pick up the bodies, thinking all the time, "This could have been me!"

Charlie decided he had enough money to buy fencing for his forty acres of brush on a side hill, and he quit. Carl was left without a falling partner. He was sitting on his bunk wondering what to do when in strode a big Russian bucker and asked if Carl would take him on. "Sure!" said Carl, and they headed for the woods together.

A bucker saws logs lengthwise and has to push as well as pull the heavy saw through the wood. Although the job takes a good deal of strength and skill, it is very monotonous. As the saw swung back and forth eating into the wood, Carl couldn't see the Russian. But he soon noticed his new partner was both pushing and pulling, and he had nothing to do but ride the saw. Now and then the Russian's red face would come around from behind the tree, grinning, "How'm I doin', Sid?"

"Fine, you're doin' just fine."

One day the Russian cut his leg with the saw, and it bled terribly. He ran into the woods looking for a hollow tree, and came back with a handful of black cobwebs to slap on the wound. To Carl's surprise, he survived.

By the time the season came to an end, Carl had grown into a strapping young man about five feet nine and a hundred sixty pounds, with powerful arm muscles and strong, oversized, capable hands. When they said "so long," the men supposed their paths might cross again some time. But Carl never saw Charlie or the Russian or the camp at Weed again.

When he left the camp in October, 1921, Carl had saved up a thousand dollars, and once more he returned to his parents with a bulging wallet. They had moved to Los Angeles and had bought their first house. His mother wanted linoleum for the kitchen floor, a fine new kitchen cabinet, and a gas stove with a glass oven door. With Carl's savings she was able to buy them all.

Prohibition was in force, but his parents liked to have wine for dinner. Charles' great project was to dig a wine cellar under the kitchen with a trapdoor in the middle of the floor. He spent hours down there with barrels and pipettes perfecting his skill as a vintner.

Charles was now chef at the Wilshire Country Club in Hollywood. Uncle Hermann was working with him, and Carl signed on as *garde manger*. Fresh out of the camps, he was back in the realm of haute cuisine, helping to fill *vols au vent* with delicate concoctions, and constructing memorable galantines of pâté filled with forcemeat and whole truffles, ornamented with green pistachio nuts, rolled in cloth, and cooked in consomme.

Again, Carl would not last at this indoor life. The mountains beckoned.

7
Decision at Big Bear Lake

Back in 1920, Carl's association with Jim Wyllie had a profound effect on his attitude toward learning and school. He was intensely curious about the workings of the natural world and was beginning to realize he couldn't learn it all on his own. While they were at Caribou, Jim had told him, "Those plants you want to know, just be patient and you will. They've all been bottled, baled, and tagged long ago. You'll find out what they are some day. You should go back to school."

Another time in the camps, one of the older men had grabbed Carl's arm and pointed to his own head. "You see these gray hairs?"

"What about them?"

"The only good they are to me now is when I hop a freight, the brakie doesn't knock me off with his brake stick." Then he added, "Slim, you go to school."

Though Carl yearned to read, he found little except dime novels and pulp magazines in the camps. One day in Butt Valley while working near a little schoolhouse, he peered through the window and saw a shelf of books. He slid his hand along the window frame, gave a slight push, and discovered it wasn't locked.

That night he returned to the schoolhouse with a lantern, climbed in the window, and selected a volume. At dawn the next morning he returned it, and came back in the evening to borrow another. In this way he read Washington Irving, James Fenimore Cooper, and other writers popular in classrooms of the day. Carl's intellectual horizons were once more expanding.

After leaving the camps, while staying with his parents in Los Angeles Carl began exploring the nearby mountains. By now he was calling many of the plants by their Latin names, and sketching almost as much as writing. "Erosion," he wrote, "to a casual observer, has not done anything unusual in our world. But could he have lived long enough, and having known these mountains when they were young, then returned to visit them a geologic hour later, shrunk beyond recognition, carved into a thousand gorges and canyons, crumbling knife-blade ridges, and bristling peaks, how surprised he would be!"

In October, 1921, starting on a three day trip to climb Mount San Antonio northwest of San Bernardino, he wrote, "Light of heart, and free, I set out this morning. Gads! My nerves are fine! Bees can walk on my hand and I am not disturbed!"

Later that fall his Uncle Hermann found a job as cook at the Big Bear Tavern on Big Bear Lake and took Carl with him as assistant. Back to making pies, cakes, muffins, and hotcakes. Big Bear was in the Jeffrey pine forest at 6,750 feet; whatever he was doing, Carl was happy when he was in the woods.

As usual, however, grouchy Uncle Hermann found something to grouse about after a month or so, and quit at the drop of a hat. Carl, too, was out of a job.

The tavern faced a bay, and on a point of land across the lake stood a large two story log house. It was owned by two immensely wealthy brothers recently arrived from England, William and Richard Burke, who lived there with William's American wife and their four children. Everyone called Richard "Uncle Dickie." The Burkes offered Carl a job as houseboy, and he accepted. He stayed through the winter, spring, and summer of 1922.

The log house seemed like a palace with its many spacious rooms full of elegant furniture. It was run by a jolly German cook and his wife, two butlers, a nanny fresh from Ireland for the children, and Carl to step and fetch, polish the floors, and keep the fireplace replenished.

Mrs. Burke had a spoiled little pekingese who was the apple of her eye, far more coddled than her children. The dog rather terrorized Carl, snapping at his heels at every opportunity. Often during dinner Mrs. Burke would ask, "Oh, Carl, would you go get a chop for Tai Tai?" He would have to climb the snowy hill to an outbuilding, hack off a chop from a frozen lamb hanging there, and carry it to the cook to broil.

In spite of their high style, with two butlers serving the three adult Burkes at dinner, Carl was astonished at the monotonous alternation of roast beef and roast lamb in their diet, not at all like his family's continental cuisine.

In addition to polishing floors and chopping wood, Carl had the job of crossing the lake in a boat for supplies. On one such trip to the resort he witnessed a grisly and ceremonious hog-killing. He found that although he worked hard he had time for play, too. He liked to romp with the children and their nanny, who was hardly older than he. He shyly confessed to his journal some romantic feelings about the nanny.

When there was some free time, Carl hiked in the woods by himself, climbed all the nearby mountain slopes and rock formations, and made minute observations of nature which he recorded in his journal. He listed the birds, trees, and flowers, and noted the weather and the position of the con-stellations. Plants he couldn't name, he sketched. He was studying the grasses and took a great interest in the structures of their blossoms. One day he dis-covered an especially large and beautiful sugar pine tree, and later he led William and Uncle Dickie to see and photograph it. William, something of a dandy, dressed very grandly in plus-fours, toting a large camera and an umbrella.

In late October Carl climbed Mount San Gorgonio in a snow storm. On the upper slopes he found ice crystals extended from the tips of every needle of the Jeffrey pines like clusters of white stilettos.

On his days off he went into the nearby town of Pine Knot to the public library. He carried off all of Muir's books ("not to read but just to steal a look into now and then"), Van Dyke's *The Desert, Elements of Geology* by Joseph Le Conte, and above all, Sudworth's *Forest Trees of the Pacific Slope*, a publica-tion of the United States Forest Service. This last was his textbook for the winter. Each evening he copied page after page in his best hand. Carl was determined not only to learn all the trees, but to understand their characteris-tics, their habitats — as we would say now, their ecology. From time to time as he copied, he would lift his head to listen to a plaintive little bird song that seemed to call him from the forest.

Carl did not neglect poetry. He read the *Complete Poems of Robert Burns*, and spent some time over Coleridge. Fascinated by his "Hymn Before Sunrise in the Vale of Chamouni," he copied several versions of it. Coleridge addresses Mont Blanc:

> "O dread and silent Mount! I gazed upon thee,
> Till thou, still present to the bodily sense,
> Didst vanish from my thought; entranced in prayer
> I worshipped the Invisible alone."

The poem echoed Carl's own feelings. He, like Coleridge and Muir, found divinity in the beauties of the natural world, and often spoke of "the godful forest" in his journals.

It was a heavy winter that year. When the lake froze and the snow drifted high, Carl circled Big Bear Lake on snowshoes pulling a toboggan to bring home the supplies. He loved these excursions through the winter wonderland, the slide of snowshoes across powdery snow, the chirping of occasional birds, the voice of the wind in the pines. He often got up early just to see it all. He recorded in his notebook, "I am seeping and soaking in Grand Nature, learning love-lessons every day without knowing it." Early one snowy morning he found a corner of the lake covered with ice as clear as glass. He ran back to get his ice skates and for a shining hour skimmed across the gleaming surface. No one was about, and the only sound was the swish-swish of his skates on the polished ice.

As spring came on and late snow storms blanketed the hills, Carl began to notice more birdsong, the swelling of buds, the sound of streams thawing under the snow. On March 14th he climbed one of the nearby peaks and wrote, "Using the tail of my snowshoes as a staff, thrusting it into the snow as a precaution against the deep crevices that abound between the summit rocks on descending, I noticed the strange deep shadowy blue of the holes in the snow I had made. I had read of blue-snow-shadows long before, but this is the first time it was shown to me so startlingly clear."

Uncle Dickie, then in his late twenties, was everyone's favorite. Occasionally he took Carl out in the big McFarland automobile and taught him how to drive. Dickie was an intellectual and an ascetic who slept in a small room as bare as a monk's cell with a single cot and a shelf of books. While polishing Dickie's bedroom floor, Carl looked at the books and was impressed to see Tolstoy, Ouspensky, and Francis Bacon's *Novum Organum* in Latin. He borrowed Thoreau's *Walden*. Reading the chapter, "The Pond in Winter," he felt a deep resonance with his own experience, and wondered if someday he might be as scholarly as Uncle Dickie and as eloquent as Thoreau.

In Pine Knot, Carl got to know Ervin Thompson, a jolly young high school science teacher who was interested in botany. They began taking hikes together, and the teacher shared with Carl what he knew of plants and other natural history. Ervin showed him a fascinating marsh full of rare plants. Yet Carl could never bring himself to confide his secret desire to study.

The weather grew warmer, a channel opened in the icy lake, and at last the ice melted altogether. Carl and Ervin spent one evening after work searching for snow plants, but couldn't find any. The next morning Carl discovered several quite near the house. Perhaps these vivid red shoots signaled a new direction. He felt that somehow he was about to make a change. Contrasting the

possibilities of learning and culture with life in the woods, he realized the latter was a dead end, and school was the only answer. School — where all the
plants were bottled, baled, and tagged, and books came by the hundreds
instead of by twos and threes.

On June 6th, Carl climbed Sugar Loaf with Thompson, having one
delightful flower encounter after another. "Shall never forget my first meeting
with the real blue violet with the heart shaped leaves. Thompson also showed
me some blue eyed grass and meadow rue." Higher up, he saw his first limber
pine.

On the descent they heard a thrush singing, "the same song that has awed
me in the Plumas forests...its song, heard in the deep, still mountain forests, is
enough to make anyone not wholly apathetic stand still, open eyed and silent,
and think of God."

In late June he took a weekend off to visit his parents. He backpacked
along the mountain range, spending the night in the neglected vegetable garden of a lonely deserted house. Next day in Los Angeles he bought himself a
second-hand set of the *Harvard Classics* and a dictionary: accoutrements of
the student he planned to be.

Back at Big Bear Lake, Carl told Dickie of his decision to continue his education. Dickie, though sorry to see him leave, applauded the decision.

The proper way to start, Carl thought, was to have a good long hike in the
mountains. On August 30th he rolled up his blankets in a bindle, said goodby
to the Burkes, and cut off through the woods to meet Mr. Thompson. After
camping on Glass Creek, they continued to the base of Mount San Gorgonio
and camped again. Their dinner was corn dodgers, rice pudding, and hot
chocolate — "very fine." The next morning they climbed to the summit of
Mount San Gorgonio; on the slopes Carl was pleased to meet red heather for
the first time "emitting a most delicious odor — the mountains' own flower."

They followed the divide over Mounts Jepson and Charlton and made
another discovery, a bank of red snow colored by the algae that inhabited it.
After a third night out they searched for a glacier they had heard about, but
night fell before they found it. Up at dawn, they finally located the glacier.
"The ice is nearly wasted, but...it has been very destructive in the past winter I
presume; many trees have been torn and broken and lying in heaps from the
weight of the slipping snow...It is a little baby — a charming little thing. A
mild winter and it will disappear."

Again they climbed upward, and about noon reached the summit of
Mount San Bernardino. From this last conquest they plunged sliding down

the mountain through talus, chinquapin, yellow pines, and chaparral. They enjoyed one last camp before reaching the orange groves and walking to San Bernardino, where Carl took the trolley home to Los Angeles.

Once home, he set out to find a school that would accept him. On September 11, 1922, he was enrolled as a ninth grade student in the new Le Conte Junior High School. He was nineteen. His life would never be the same again.

Over sixty years later, Uncle Dickie turned on his television set to watch the "Over Easy" show on public television and saw Carl in a special feature as a ranger naturalist leading a flower walk in Yosemite Valley. "That's our Carl!" he said to himself, and promptly wrote his old friend and houseboy a letter. Carl was delighted to hear from him, and in the spring of 1985 they saw each other again in Los Angeles. Carl was eighty-two and Uncle Dickie almost ninety.

They had arranged to meet for lunch at the California Institute of Technology, of which Burke was a patron. As Carl waited, a Rolls Royce drove up, and a tall dignified old gentleman with a cane got out. Overcome with the memory of what Uncle Dickie had been to him, Carl embraced him fondly. Over lunch at the Athanaeum, Dickie showed Carl pictures of his son, one of the designers of the famous human-propelled ultra-light plane, the Gossamer Albatross. He also shared a book about his ancestor, one of three Burke brothers who had come out from Ireland to San Francisco in the 1860's and started its industrial development. San Francisco dedicated a monument to their memory.

This meeting with Uncle Dickie was a precious moment to Carl. It brought back his distant youth and the momentous decision he had made at Big Bear Lake.

The Long Growing

8
Finding the Trail with Harry James

"I took the trail less traveled by,
And that has made all the difference."
—Robert Frost

C arl was now nineteen years old, experienced in the ways of the woods but rather naive as to higher education. At Le Conte Junior High School he felt himself a man among children. Yet he was so keen to learn that he didn't worry about age difference, and the other students accepted and liked him. With his naturally cheerful disposition and inclination to work hard and obey rules, he made a niche of his own.

Nowadays he would not be required to attend junior and senior high schools. A few adult education courses plus the state high school proficiency exam would quickly bring him a diploma, and he would be off to college. In 1922 this was not the case, and he doggedly set himself to the treadmill.

Carl excelled in English and scientific subjects, but math had been neglected in his program of self-education in the camps. It irked him to see other ninth graders sail through the mysteries of algebra while he bumped along behind. In time he got the hang of it, but mathematics was never one of his enthusiasms.

His parents offered no objection to his going back to school, but neither did they encourage him. They had assumed Carl had put schooling behind him and was now a self-supporting adult. But though they may have thought he was taking a step backward, the bond between the three of them was strong and deep. Where understanding failed, loyalty took over.

For a while he lived at home again, but when he started working at the Wilshire Country Club he lived at the club. Charles, who had become a well-known chef by this time, had gone on to a position as Secretary of the Chefs de Cuisine Association of California. The Association was a kind of employment agency for chefs, who enjoyed considerable prestige but were never paid

what they were worth. All of Carl's life the family was in moderate circumstances.

From Hollywood in those vivid smog-free days Carl could see the mountains on the skyline. He climbed Camelback several times. In Muir's writings,
which he never ceased enjoying, he read of the waterfall and "the flowers, the
bees, the ferny rocks and leafy shade forming a charming little poem of
wilderness,...extending down the flowery slopes of Mount San Antonio
through the rugged, foam-beaten bosses of the main Eton Canyon."

Drawn by a desire to find this little paradise, Carl bought a map, and on his
first free weekend he found himself on the route. Houses followed him about
half the distance, then came vineyards as he began climbing upward.

The hillside soon turned into a steep wall along a knife-edge that led into a
little dell with deep pools shaded by broad-leaved maples and alders.
Maidenhair ferns nodded in the rock fissures, and wild sage and other "bee
flowers" grew everywhere. The rugged canyon was little changed since
Muir's day.

Charmed with this secret wilderness, Carl returned again and again, bringing his blankets with him and staying overnight. On the way home, thirsty
and hungry, he would slip into a vineyard and lie on the ground feasting on
grapes. He reasoned that it wasn't stealing if he took none away, and anyhow
the tiny quantity he consumed was hardly noticeable.

Occasionally in Eton Canyon he met a handsome, stylish young man
dressed in a broad-brimmed Stetson hat and knickers, always accompanied by
a group of boys. His name was Harry James. How portentous these chance
meetings would be, and how much they would change Carl's life — or rather,
intensify the channel he had already marked out for himself!

Harry was a Canadian journalist who had come to Hollywood in its early
days, had acted in Griffith's "The Birth of a Nation," and was acquainted
with many early actors like Lillian Gish and the Barrymores. In addition to
the movies, he had numerous other interests, among them conservation.
With the help of his close friend, Paul G. Redington of the National Forest
Service, James was instrumental in the establishment of the San Gorgonio
Wilderness Area.

Harry could have led a leisured life, but he was imbued with a deep desire
to share culture and adventure with boys. He had met an old Penobscot
Indian, Dark Cloud, on a movie set. They began hiking together in the hills
along with various boys who were thrilled by the presence of a real live
Indian. Harry also knew Ernest Thompson Seton, the celebrated naturalist

Harry James.

Carl in Trailfinders' Camp, 1921.

and outdoorsman. Under Seton's guidance he started a boys' organization affiliated with Seton's Woodcraft League of America.

The League was given permission to use Le Conte Junior High for their weekly evening meetings. There Harry met Carl again, conspicuous among the younger students. Before long, Harry had heard all about this young man who had returned to school after a life in the woods, and he encouraged Carl to come around to the meetings.

One evening while the boys were playing games, Harry and Carl strolled along the street. "Look," Harry said, "I need help. If you'll come into the group as a leader, I can pay you a small salary because the Community Chest gives me some funds." Carl jumped at this chance to become modestly self-supporting. Best of all, he could be part of this wonderful organization.

He worked with Harry at least seven years, as the club grew from a single group or council to ten councils of fifty boys each in various sections of the city. Apparently James and Seton didn't see eye to eye on some matters. As Harry had a quick temper and a stern sense of the rightness of his purpose, he withdrew from Seton's Western Woodcraft League to form the Western Rangers, taking most of the boys with him. They chose a horned buffalo as their totem. Eventually they changed the name to Trailfinders under the sign of a Hopi sun symbol. The Hopi sun was part of Carl's secret cosmology for the rest of his life.

Harry had a remarkable gift for working with boys of twelve or thirteen, while Carl excelled with the high schoolers. The organization was not a salvage effort for underprivileged boys. On the contrary, it was elitist. But although many of the members had money and illustrious connections, each one had to measure up as a gentleman or he was booted out forthwith.

For Carl, association with Harry was a joy beyond belief. Harry was his model, his mentor, and his friend. By being one of his leaders, Carl had the opportunity to meet many of Harry's friends who were members of the intellectual and social elite.

One of these was James Willard Schultz, famous for his books on his life among the Blackfoot Indians. When Harry was growing old he set to work on Schultz's biography, but he died before completing the work.

Another friend was Charles Fletcher Lummis, severe and colorful folklorist and archeologist of the American Southwest. Lummis had a magnificent hacienda where he would walk up and down dressed in a red banda, turquoise beads, a sash, and thick corduroy trousers, smoking a vile cigar as he dictated to a secretary. He taught the boys Spanish songs of the New Mexico frontier.

One memorable evening, Carl had dinner with the Barrymores.

During the school year, the boys were off with their packs every Friday at the end of classes. They took the trolley to the end of the line and headed up the trails into the San Gabriels and San Bernardinos. On one trip, 150 boys climbed to the top of Mount San Gorgonio and had a gigantic campout at Dry Lake. Carl ended up carrying six boys' packs. When they came to a frozen snowbank descending into a small lake, a bunch of the boys stripped and slid down the slick snow into the water for a swim.

Gradually the Trailfinders were becoming a seasoned crew of young outdoorsmen. As they scoured the nearby mountains, Carl derived the keenest pleasure from their expeditions.

9
School & Work

"Life without industry is guilt; Industry without Art is Brutality."
— John Ruskin

So wrote Carl in his journal, as he plugged away in school. After only a fall semester at junior high, where he did well, he was off to Lincoln High School. He chose it because a number of the Trailfinders were students there.

His grades had been good, but they began to fluctuate. He threw himself into literature and science, which fascinated him, and his Latin teacher was a peach. But the chemistry course was weak and dull, and he found it difficult to grind on geometry and trigonometry. He had his eye on the long haul, not on petty day-to-day tasks. The principal, a big red-haired woman named Ethel Percy Andrus (she would later achieve some fame as founder of the American Association of Retired Persons), called him on the carpet several times, and he had a feeling she didn't like him. Perhaps it was true. The unusual can be a thorn in the side of some educators who find it easier to deal with peas in a pod.

On many evenings, he supervised a Trailfinders' council at the school. Every council elected a chief, and at each meeting the chief called on one boy to recite the laws which had been written by Harry James. The boy would stand and say:

"Oh Chief, be courageous physically, mentally and morally. Be clean in mind and body. Be honorable. Hold your word as sacred. Be reverent. Be respectful of all worship of the Great Spirit, the Master of Life. Be kind to all living things. Be loyal, for loyalty is the foundation of friendship, and friendships are among the choice things in life. Be truthful not only in word but in thought. Seek diligently for the truth to be found in all things. Be wise, for stupidity is the root of all evil. Be happy. Seek the joy of life to be found in simple things and in the results of good work well done!"

Thus Harry shared his idealism with the boys.

Later Harry married Grace Clifford, a teacher in one of the schools where he had a council, and together they founded The Trailfinder School for Boys in 1926, starting with about thirty students. Grace was the teacher. The school moved several times, and for a while occupied the home of writer Upton Sinclair.

While still in high school, Carl worked at The Trailfinder School as chauffeur and factotum and was given lodging in return for his services. It was fun driving Harry about in his beautiful red touring Buick with red leather upholstery. On council nights, Carl took him to one

Beth Robinson, Carl's first girlfriend, 1923.

council, went to lead another one himself, then drove back to pick up Harry. Afterwards they often attended an opera, though they invariably missed the first act. Carl was enthralled to be introduced to Harry's glamorous world.

His clothes weren't exactly up to snuff, however. His mother Marie remade his father's old suits for him, and although she was a skilled seamstress, she scorned fashion. Elegant Harry once scolded Carl about his clothes, and Carl was hurt. But with his limited resources he continued dressing as he had always done.

Harry, seeing that public schools were primarily aimed at the average student, wanted The Trailfinder School to serve boys with the highest ability. He established a challenging intellectual curriculum, and at the same time instilled in his students his philosophy of health, social responsibility, and love of nature. He constantly stressed discrimination and good taste, and what he called character.

He devised a natty school uniform: bronze corduroy knickers, gray knee socks, a blue flannel shirt, and a regimental Scottish-Canadian tam o' shanter. On trips, the boys wore blue jeans, red bandana handkerchiefs, and Stetson hats with handmade horsehair hatbands, each decorated with a silver conch. They made themselves neckerchief holders of sheep vertebrae, each formed to resemble a steer's head with inset turquoise eyes and a coral tongue.

During the school year, Carl and the boys relished visits to the Old Mission Playhouse in a ramshackle barn in San Gabriel. They attended its single play many times — a romanticized history of the Spanish in California, full of melodrama and sentiment. One episode involved the good Padre Garcés and an Indian child named Vincenzo. The Trailfinders' hearts warmed as the padre called, "Vincenzo! Vincenzo!" and the child entered and knelt, tugged at the black robe, and said in his high-pitched voice, *"Sí, padre."* They shuddered with delight when the priest foiled the wicked captain, wresting his weapon away and hurling it offstage as he shouted, "There is your sword! Go follow it!"

The boys had a drive to collect money for building a new Mission Playhouse, and Harry asked Carl to get a rock from the top of Mount San Gorgonio for a cornerstone. He floundered up the mountain in a blizzard and carried down a good big stone in his knapsack through the deep snow.

In high school Carl had one girl friend, an honor student named Beth Robinson. They walked in the mountains together and shared many interests, and he fell deeply in love with her. But being older he began to have older ideas; he wanted to get married. She was too young to consider the thought, and when they finally broke it off, Carl was so profoundly stricken that he disappeared alone for two weeks into the sheltering mountains.

It was the fall of the year, and in the San Gabriels the flowers had gone to seed. Here and there golden willow boughs or red-leaved herbs flamed against the dun grass, while the evergreens reminded him of life relatively unchanging even in the ephemeral realm of living things. He knew he would never forget Beth, but spring would come again, and the world was fundamentally right. Finally he worked through his anguish and came back down to go on with his life.

When not working with the Trailfinders, Carl was employed in restaurants or at day labor. One summer he worked in the kitchen of the Raymond Hotel in Pasadena under Chef "Monsieur Poupée." In the fall of 1929 he was working as *garde manger* at the Miramar, a stylish restaurant in Santa Monica, when he heard the news of the crash on Wall Street.

The summer before, 1928, he had worked for Caldor (California Door Division of the Diamond Match Company) near Shingle Springs in El Dorado County, cutting and milling huge sugar pines. He was chaser on the rigging slinger crew. If a log got hung up on a stump as it was being dragged to the mill, he would signal to stop the engine and back up the line so that he could free the log. He was injured once when a cable snapped up and

Carl and staff members at Big Bear Lake.

knocked him to the ground. For years afterwards his right leg hurt if pulled
or twisted.

Carl's best friend at Caldor was Bob Russell, the first "high climber" in the
state. He was a massive Hercules of a man whose job was to top trees two
hundred feet above ground. One day Carl was struggling to free a caught log,
but the cable had bitten into the wood. He broke into a sweat and kept
straining, when down the hill strode Bob. "'Smatter, Sid, can't you get her
loose?" With one powerful rip he tore the chain out of the stump, then
stomped back uphill in his heavy boots.

On the third of July that year, Carl saw women in the camps for the first
and last time. A couple of prostitutes dressed fit to kill drove up in a Ford
flivver. "Yoo-hoo, boys!" they called. "We'll see you tomorrow at Cherry
Flat!" Carl stood back abashed while the other men laughed and joked with
the women.

Caldor was the last episode in his life of lumbering. Working in the woods
had become purely parenthetical to his real summer interest, the Trailfinders'
trips.

10
Indian Country: The Coconino Trips

"Walk on a rainbow trail,
walk on a trail of song,
and all about you will be beauty."
— Navajo Song

I n the summer of 1926 Harry James came up with a plan for high
adventure: a Trailfinders' expedition to the Indian lands of the
Southwest. He called it the First Coconino Trip for the Coconino or
Cohonina, a prehistoric tribe of the region whose name survives in the
coconino sandstone of the Grand Canyon. He bought two old Dodges, loaded them with boys, equipment, spare gas, oil, and water, and headed to the
Grand Canyon with the Trailfinders. Carl served as cook, driver, and one of
the leaders.

Near the South Rim of the canyon they set up camp among the piñon
pines and junipers. When everything was shipshape, Harry said, "Each of you
boys go out by yourself and see the canyon." He didn't consider them too
young to respond to its deep mystery and magic. Carl too was enchanted,
absorbing the beauty of gold, rose and purple walls, the immensity of sky, the
great bell-like hollow reverberating with holiness.

There were four Coconino Trips all together, and later they would blend
in Carl's memory. Harry bought a Chevrolet truck with a canvas top, seats for
all the boys, and room for their gear. Copious supplies of food and water were
stowed aboard, and duffel bags draped over the headlights as they took off
into the desert on their southwest safaris.

Carl would remember hiking to the bottom of the Grand Canyon and
back. Glen Dawson, one of the younger boys, grew so tired on the climb out
that Carl carried him most of the way on his shoulders. Dawson grew up to
become a well-known Sierran climber.

And there was their trip into Havasupai Village, an Indian settlement deep
within the Grand Canyon. They started down on horseback with Carl wran-

gling the animals. Arriving in the village on a very warm afternoon, they found the Indian Agent asleep with his feet on a rail. When they asked permission to proceed, the agent woke up with a great yawn. His false teeth were held in place by a spring, but the spring was sluggish, and the boys stared in disbelief as the teeth slowly opened to meet his gaping mouth.

They continued down past an old Indian woman alternately grating corn into a bowl and whacking the mob of cats who tried to steal it. Next they met a man they irreverently named Chief Coffeepot. He was elegantly dressed in tribal fashion with a banda on his head, and the boys asked if they could take his picture. Flattered, Chief Coffeepot excused himself and dashed into his hut. Several minutes later, he emerged done out in Montgomery Wards overalls and shirt like any other rancher.

As the group descended into the canyon, Carl helped himself to the peaches growing abundantly along the trail. He had no container, so he filled the inside of his shirt with luscious ripe fruit. When some of the pack stock spooked, his horse broke into a run, the peaches slowly turning to jam as the horse pelted wildly through thorny chaparral. Carl was scratched, sticky, and grimy when they reached drooping curtains of travertine rock, passed between them as through a door, and found a natural pool. Everyone stripped down and had a glorious splashy swim in the cool water.

On another Coconino Trip the Trailfinders visited the Zuñi and Acoma Pueblos. In Zuñi they learned about the Center of the World. It seems that when the God Water Strider and his fellows created the earth, they made it flat and told the people to stay away from the edge. The foolish Zuñis ignored his warning and soon found themselves clinging to the margin about to fall off. In his mercy, Father Water Strider picked them up and set them back in the very center, and there they sensibly live to this day. They have built a sacred shrine marking the Center of the World to remind themselves where they belong.

Between Zuñi and Acoma the Trailfinders stopped at El Moro (Inscription Rock) and set up their tents at its base. When Carl went looking for firewood, there was none to be found. Big black clouds were boiling across the sky, and suddenly, as though by the magic of the Indian gods, a huge bolt of lightning hit a nearby tree and smashed it to smithereens just the right size for a campfire. In celebration Carl turned out a batch of fried crullers over the fragrant glowing coals.

For dinner music at El Moro the boys set a Victrola on a box and played Wagner. From under the rocky overhang, the music echoed beautifully in the gathering dark. They began to sing. Out of the night appeared two Basque sheepherders, charmed into their circle by the sweet sounds so rare in their lonely wandering life.

In the morning Carl got up first and started the fire. He saw a figure approaching through the sagebrush, just a head bobbing across the vast plain. Closer and closer the stranger came until he let out a hail and passed on by. It was an Indian runner on his way from Acoma to Zuñi.

Proceeding toward Acoma, the group camped at the base of the Mesa Encantada or Enchanted Mesa. Harry, a master raconteur, told how long ago some early Acomas lived on top of the mesa until a storm washed out their route. Unable to get down, they were condemned to slow starvation. The boys hunched close to their fire in the dark, thinking of those ancient Indians dying together, while flashes of lightning lit up the mesa like a great ghost.

When they reached Acoma, the City in the Sky, the Trailfinders clambered up a steep ancient trail to the top. On the mesa there are no springs, and rain-water had to be channeled into natural cisterns in the rocks. Carl lay down on his belly to stare at some brine shrimp in one of them. Suddenly, plop! He was deluged with water. As he came up spluttering he heard musical laughter, and saw the bank of the cistern lined with Acoma women. One had thrown a rock in, and all were covering their mouths Indian fashion so as to hide their laughter.

As they walked the streets of the old village, the boys saw that the Indians still used sheets of gypsum instead of glass for windowpanes. Harry retold the story (from Willa Cather's *Death Comes for the Archbishop*) of the wicked priest who cruelly mistreated the Acomas. He was finally taken by the head and heels and, without a word spoken, was hurled over the edge of the mesa to his death.

On one of their expeditions the Trailfinders went to Zion Canyon. Carl had not yet seen Yosemite, but in later years he would notice the resemblance between these two lovely narrow valleys surrounded by stupendous cliffs. But Zion's cliffs are glowing red and yellow, the petrified record of millions of years of shifting sands now cross-bedded sandstone, while Yosemite is carved of solid gray granite.

From Zion, their truck bumped along among the magnificent firs, pines, spruce, and aspens on the high Kaibab Plateau and crawled down the steep track to the Colorado River with all brakes smoking. At Lee's Ferry they crossed on the rickety ferry, then climbed a narrow road with no guardrails, two thousand feet up along the canyon walls to Tuba City. Nearby they saw

Music appreciation with Carl on Coconino Trip.

dinosaur tracks in the rocks looking as fresh as though the great reptiles had passed only a minute before. They completed the circle by returning to the North Rim of the Grand Canyon.

These were the years when the deer had multiplied greatly and cropped the forest clean as high as they could reach. It was thought they could be herded into other areas, and every cowpoke in the country came to a great roundup. The roundup failed. Later the Park Service realized that the deer population was out of balance because of the killing-off of predators like mountain lions and coyotes, and the service itself reduced the number of deer in order to save the forest

The greatest event of the Coconino Trips was going to Hopiland. Harry James, whose lifelong interest in Indians led to his founding the Indian Welfare League and the National Association to Help the Indian, was well known among the Hopis. He had once used his influence to engineer the dismissal of a detested Indian Agent, and the Hopis never forgot it. They called him Honauwayma, Walking Bear, and welcomed him whenever he came.

In those days there were no decent roads in Hopiland. The expedition had to drive up washes and across sandy wastes. Summer storms often threatened washouts which could efface the route and endanger their very lives with flash floods. When they stopped at a wooden hogan and asked a Navajo the way, the Indian stared enigmatically and made a circular motion over half the horizon in answer.

When they reached the old Hopi pueblo of Oraibi, the boys camped below the mesa. The aromatic desert plants, the vast spaces and clear silent air,

Carl with Trailfinders on the Dana Glacier, 1943.

and the Indians moving about their business talking cheerfully among themselves in their own language, all filled Carl with a great peace. He started a list
of Hopi words and phrases in his little black book.

Old Tewaquaptewa had been chief for years and years, back to the time
when the Hopis of Oraibi had had a great quarrel. The chief had brought out
a rope and traced a line in the dust with a stick. "Well, it has to be this way,
that when you pass over this line, it will be done," he said. Then all the men
of the village had a tug-of-war, and those who were pulled over the line had
to go away and make the new town of Hotevilla. When Carl visited, the quarrel was long gone but not forgotten. The wound in the social fabric of Oraibi
remained as a sorrow.

One evening, Chief Tewaquaptewa, who had composed many songs, invited the Trailfinders to a song fest. As the sun was going down, the Crier Chief
came out on a rooftop and announced in Hopi that the white boys were
coming to the chief's house for a sing. Rather shy and quiet, the boys climbed
the log ladders to a roof of the house where the chief lived. The chief's wife
brought out piles of sheep skins, and the Trailfinders settled down on the soft
skins and leaned against the walls.

Slowly the night began to fall and the men to arrive. A figure appeared at
the top of the ladder and seated himself in a corner, then another and another
until there were about thirty men. They were dressed in loose white cotton
trousers and shirts of their own weaving, and wore bandas around their
heads. On wrists, in earlobes, and around necks hung heavy turquoises.

When it was fully dark, Chief Tewaquaptewa came out of the house dressed in his best buckskins, turquoises, and an eagle feather, and bearing a huge cottonwood log drum. He seated himself quietly and began to beat the drum and sing while the men joined in. The songs went on and on with endless variations and many strange and beautiful minor notes. There was no conversation. Now and then one of the men rolled a Bull Durham cigarette, and Carl could see his strong and serene features in the flash of match-light. In the warm, balmy summer darkness, the whole house vibrated with the hollow sound of the drum.

After a long time the songs ended and died away. One by one the men rose and disappeared down the ladder into the dark without a single word to break the spell.

Some time after that, Chief Tewaquaptewa visited Harry James in Los Angeles. Carl drove them through the city to see the sights, but the chief stared straight ahead and looked neither right nor left. Only when the ocean came in view did he react with awe and joy. At last, here was the Mother of Waters which he had heard of but never seen. Reverently, he took out a bag of cornmeal, sprinkled some on the sand where the waves came in, and offered up a prayer.

The Coconino Trips entered powerfully into Carl's understanding of the natural world. He became deeply aware of the layers of sediment deposited slowly and inexorably through millions of years to build up the land, and then just as slowly and inexorably eroded into canyons. Glowing sandstone, dark wavy petrified wood, and precious fossils of ancient life pressed into stone, all astounded and thrilled him. Humbled by the vastness and drawn into the web of beauty, he thought it a great thing to study the history of the earth.

The plants too, harsh and soft, aromatic and fetid, brilliantly colored or blending their hues to the hues of stone and sand, filled him with delight.

Not least were the Indians whom he came to respect and admire for their close social ties, their strange evocative rituals, and their mythology. Their stories spoke to him of the oneness of nature, man, and man's gods in a way that he had dimly felt, but seldom found expressed in western literature with such simple power and conviction. Ever afterwards he would feel drawn to this enchanted world where Coyote Person and Raven Person and Rabbit Person circle with man and flower and star and sky in the endless dance of creation.

11
The Trail Leads to the Sierra

"Give me health and a day, and I will make the pomp of emperors ridiculous."
— Ralph Waldo Emerson

Carl's council of older boys had cut their teeth backpacking in the San Gabriels and the San Bernardinos. On their trips they had a campfire every evening, sometimes a formal council with recitation of the Trailfinder Laws. Carl might give a "ranger report" — a little talk about natural history. Each boy would follow by contributing some anecdote or observation. Once the famous naturalist Enos Mills visited a council and listened to these Trailfinder reports. "I feel as if I had a dozen pairs of eyes and ears to see and listen for me at a dozen different places. What an excellent way to stimuate and train in observation!" he wrote. After the reports the Trailfinders sang songs of their own or Harry's composition. One had a chorus that began: "Climb the mountains, climb the mountains, Gain the freedom they so freely give!" The boy with the honor of lighting the fire had the responsibility of putting it out at evening's end.

In 1927, Carl's group decided to take on the Sierra. Excited evenings were devoted to manufacturing gear and dehydrating food. They specialized in beans pre-cooked and oven-dried, later to be converted to soups and stews on the trail. They also cured jerky, dried prunes and apples, and evolved a flapjack mix which would serve for both breakfasts and lunches. A few slabs of bacon, salami and cheese, some Klim (dried whole milk), and a lemonade concentrate completed their commissary. Each boy would carry and cook his own food.

Carl designed a pack with a tumpline modeled on the Poirier Pack used in the old north woods. It was a huge rectangular sack of heavy canvas with a flap. Later he added a packframe of spruce wood with curved crossbars and heavy belting across the small of the back.

The Trailfinders had no sleeping bags but used blankets with horse-blanket pins. The sleeping rolls were heavy and not as warm as they might have been.

Without groundsheets or pads, the boys depended on pine needles to warm their beds. Carl soon learned that Jeffrey and whitebark duff made good mattresses, but a night under a lodgepole pine was cold and prickly. To stay warmer he bought himself an expensive "Woods Arctic Eiderdown Sleeping Robe" advertised in *Field and Stream* for sixty dollars. It weighed thirteen pounds. Luxury at last! He labeled it in India ink along the border with his Hopi name (Niwipnimtewa or Climber of Mountains), the date (1925), and his totem (a round mountain with steps going up it.) Underneath, he drew Indian sign language depicting a five days' march with a campfire at the end of each day, and halfway through, a mountain.

Scorning Boy Scout cook-kits, the boys learned from Carl to make nested pots of tin cans with haywire bails, and tin can lanterns like the one old Jim Wyllie had made in the big woods. He also taught them to drive hobnails into their boots for climbing in snow.

On a summer night in 1927, Carl and five carefully selected boys boarded a midnight train in Los Angeles, bound for Bishop and the Sierra Nevada. By dawn they could see the magnificent Sierran scarp rising to the west. They watched euphorically, debating where to start on their hike. The amused conductor kept asking, "Mountains high enough for you? Wait a while."

They waited as long as they could stand it. When the train made a short stop south of Lone Pine, they got off. As they trudged across the desert toward the mountains, three armed men rose out of the brush: ranchers at war with the Los Angeles Water Department, trying with guns to prevent the diversion of water from the Sierra streams that gave them irrigation. They gave the boys a good scare, but recognized they were harmless and let them go.

Carl had cut a topographic map of the entire Sierra into squares and glued the squares onto a strip of cheesecloth in such a fashion that he could fold and unfold the cloth without damaging the map. It was about seven feet long and when unrolled on a mountaintop flew out like a Tibetan prayer flag. Consulting the map, he saw that they could follow up Cottonwood Creek and enter the high country over Army Pass.

For years Carl had loved Muir's Range of Light, and now, at twenty-four years of age, he was finally seeing it with his own eyes. The blue intensity of sky, the grandeur of cliffs, the clarity of streams and the brilliance of waterfalls — he felt he had been here before, that he had always been here, that he belonged.

He had learned many plants in the mountains down south, but here he entered the true world of alpine flora. As his rugged work boots plodded upward, he noticed buckwheats and heathers, epilobiums and lupines — familiar genera, but most species still nameless to him. He slept under the whitebark pine and counted stars through its needles. He saw the foxtail pine clutching at rocks and cliffs and waving in the wind. He walked in boggy meadows of heavenly green. He smelled wild onion, pennyroyal, and mountain sagebrush. He was happy.

The boys climbed Mounts Guyot, Whitney, and Tyndall. At a mountain lake near Whitney, Carl fished for the first time with a willow pole and some captured flies. The golden trout came swarming and he shortly had enough for dinner. When he took the beautiful gold-speckled fish in his hands, he felt a twinge of guilt. It seemed a shame to kill these beautiful harmless creatures. Nevertheless, they tasted great.

It had been a very snowy year, and the snow still lingered. One afternoon in a heavy mist the boys floundered through drifts and slipped on icy patches all the way from Tyndall Creek over Harrison Pass. About dark, they began struggling downhill through willow thickets toward East Lake, looking for a place to camp. Below their feet was a constant gurgling of water running under the snowbound willow branches. Suddenly on the opposite slope they saw the orange glow of a small campfire. Hurrying toward it they discovered a solitary mountaineer snug by his fire in a thicket of whitebark pine, doping his boots. It was Norman Clyde, who would come to be known as the most fabulous mountaineer the Sierra has ever seen.

"Come on in, boys," he called. "You'll need two campfires, one that's bright to cook by, and one that'll last to keep you warm." They didn't wait to be asked twice before lighting up and starting their dinner. After the boys had gone to bed, Carl and Norman sat up far into the night talking about climbing.

The boys planned to climb Mount Brewer. The next morning Clyde gave them directions before they continued on their way north. He was headed south, and they never met him again. But another year on top of the North Palisade they found a scrappy little book with Clyde's signature stuffed in a can. It contained a series of messages: "Up July 10th, East Face. July 14, up the SW arrete. July 20, up the West Side," and so on. He had climbed it day after day by every possible route.

As they came down Vidette Creek, the stream was very high. The boys struggled across in single file. Suddenly the last one in the line slipped and went down. For a moment things looked bad, as the angry waters threatened

A group of Trailfinders with Mr. Newman, 1930.

to wash him away. In the nick of time Carl was able to grab him and pull him
to safety.

After the ascent of Mount Brewer, the Trailfinders made a big circuit down
the South Fork of the Kings River and thence over JO Pass working westward. Eventually they reached a ridge and looked down over the west slope
forest. Carl pointed, "Look at those trees with their dome-like tops rising up
like green cumulus clouds. They're the giant sequoias." Since none of them
had ever seen the big trees, they dropped down to spend a night in the shadows of the giants. At the end of their loop they hiked all the way to the
Central Valley where Mr. Newman, an old man Harry had hired, picked them
up with his truck.

From that time on, part of every summer was devoted to the Sierra. Carl
envisioned that, beginning in the south, they should cross the range by every
route from east to west and west to east, gradually working north until they
had explored its entire length. On each trip he insisted they start at the very
base of the range in order to see all the life zones from the chaparral to the
alpine fell fields.

Each summer's expedition lasted two weeks, and it took about a week to
get ready. It is to be noted that the boys had neither tents nor ground sheets.
Those were dry years, and on four summer expeditions it never rained.

In 1928 they entered from the west side, starting at Hume and going up
the South Fork of the Kings River to the Boulder Creek Sequoia Grove and
into Paradise Valley. They proceeded to Rae Lakes and climbed Black
Mountain. Descending to Vidette Meadows they climbed East Vidette, then
went up to Bullfrog Lake and out over Kearsarge Pass to Independence.

On the second morning of the hike they met a Forest Service employee and realized they had forgotten to get a fire permit. "Well, go ahead but just lay low," he advised. But Carl's stern sense of obligation made him tell the boys, "Make camp here, and I'll go back for a permit." After trotting eighteen miles up one ridge and down another, he finally reached a telephone. A voice came on the line, and Carl explained his dilemma. There was a moment of silence as the supervisor realized he was being asked to condone something he'd rather know nothing about. Then he exploded. "Go anyway," he spluttered, "but damn you!"

Carl got back to camp exhausted and found that the boys had eaten up half the grub. They made the rest of the trip on short rations.

That night they spread out over the area of an old lumber camp to build their fires and throw down their beds. During the night Carl woke to stare up at the stars, and suddenly a red hot spark blew past him. He hurried uphill to find Allen Cameron sound asleep with the thick forest litter smoking around him. Carl shook him awake. "Allen, you're burning up the forest!" The ledge where Allen had built his fire was really a dead sequoia, and the fire had eaten into the wood. Together they worked several hours with a little tin bucket to put it out.

In 1929 the Trailfinders hiked by way of Crown Valley to Tehipite Valley and Palisade Basin. They attempted to climb the North Palisade but couldn't find the right route to the top. Then over Bishop Pass and down to Big Pine to meet Mr. Newman.

In 1930, the group crossed over Paiute Pass to Humphreys Basin, where they made the difficult ascent of Mount Humphreys, and on to Evolution Basin, Glacier Divide, and Dusy Basin. Not only did they do the tough climb of Mount Darwin, but this time they succeeded in reaching the summit of North Palisade, and came out again over Bishop Pass.

Allen Cameron was very forgetful, and that summer he forgot what day the Trailfinders were leaving Los Angeles. When he realized he had missed them, he got their itinerary from Carl's mother, hustled up to the mountains, and traveled on the double to catch up. In late afternoon when the hikers were setting up camp in Dusy Basin, a tiny figure appeared in a notch on the skyline between Agassiz Needle and the next mountain. They heard a faint shout, "Vincenzo! Vincenzo!"

"*Sí, Padre!*" the boys shouted in unison, and Allen came down and joined them. He knew they would be at exactly this point at exactly this time.

Each year after two weeks of extremely rugged hiking and climbing, they returned to civilization. "Why," one of the boys asked, "is the end of our trip like a wedding?" When no one could guess, he gave the answer: "Because there's nothing left but rice and old shoes."

Yes, they were hungry. Yet they had an unwritten law: when they reached the fleshpots, no stops for junk food. (They didn't call it that, but it's what they meant.) Down from the last pass, they would march with set faces past Parcher's Camp and its tantalizing signs, "Hershey Bars, Candy, Peanuts, Coca Cola." At the roadhead Mr. Newman would be waiting. The boys would heave their now-lightened packs into the truck, climb aboard, and go off to Ma's Place in Independence for a feast — all they could eat for fifty cents apiece. One year they drove all the way to the Fred Harvey restaurant in Mohave for their celebration.

During those years, Carl stored up rich memories and an intimate knowledge of the ways of the mountains. Already an expert woodsman, he led his group not only along the main trails, but cross-country up side canyons and over little-used passes, and they climbed many of the highest peaks. The John Muir Trail was not yet completed, although they followed it where it existed. Carl noticed how high in altitude the Jeffrey pine grew, how far south the hemlock extended, the northern limits of the foxtail pine, and gathered many other bits of information that formed part of his growing knowledge of Sierran botany.

The human ties were also deep and enduring. Trailfinders had reunions and kept in touch with him down the years. When they got together they talked of the old days, the days Carl did so much to enrich. And it would be difficult to exaggerate the influence of his long, close friendship with Harry James. Harry exposed him to a world of social polish and intellectual achievement, and gave him the faith in himself to pursue both values.

Carl's role in the organization during the impressionable period of his late adolescence and early adulthood set a pattern for his future. His model had been the young John Muir who wrote of lonely wanderings and climbs. In Trailfinders, Carl discovered the satisfactions of leadership, enjoying the outdoors in the company of others whom he could guide and teach. This pattern prefigured his future as a ranger naturalist.

By the summer of 1930 the Trailfinders had arrived at the section just south of the Minarets. Carl would never reach the Minarets, for he now entered upon a new life, a life that would bind him forever to the Sierra and to Tuolumne Meadows in the high country of Yosemite National Park.

12
Yosemite at Last!

"Now I shall have another baptism,
I shall dip my soul in the high sky.
I shall go up through the pines and firs,
Among the wind waves on the mountains."
— John Muir

Meanwhile, Carl finished two years of high school and in 1928 entered Pasadena Junior College. Under the influence of Muir, he had become fascinated by glaciation and decided to major in geology. He also took his first course in botany under Miss Margaret Stason, whom he greatly respected. Her quiet appreciation of her chosen field began to draw him in that direction.

In those days, botany students spent long tedious hours at their microscopes making detailed drawings. As the hours went by, Carl felt the urge for a smoke — quite against the rules. He had learned to chew tobacco in the lumber camps during fire season when smoking was forbidden, and he tried it in the lab. Now and then he slipped over to the sink to wet his specimen and furtively spit. He thought his habit went undetected, but years later he learned that the other students had known it all the time.

After two years in junior college, Carl continued at The University of California at Los Angeles. Exploring various fields, he took astronomy and an excellent course in ornithology from Dr. Loye Holmes Miller. Dr. Miller was a whiz who could look at a bird bone, modern or fossil, and immediately identify the bird and tell when it had lived.

Carl studied mineralogy and the geology of North America. Yet he was coming to feel that geology was not to be his field after all. Much as he loved the solid earth of rock and soil and running water, he loved even more its garment of life. His earlier interest in plants prevailed, and he switched his major to botany.

He had long wished to learn the botany of the Sierra and had planned the

Trailfinder trips with that purpose in mind. He found only one book to help him: Smiley's *A Report Upon the Boreal Flora of the Sierra Nevada of California* — a good, thorough tome but hardly a field guide. As a budding botanist he studied it assiduously, building on his familiarity with the plants toward what would eventually be an immense and detailed knowledge.

In the spring of 1930 he heard about the Yosemite School of Field Natural History and applied for entrance. Only a small, select group, usually graduate students and teachers or professionals, was chosen for six weeks of concentrated field study. Carl had not yet finished college, but his grades were good, his recommendations excellent. At first named as an alternate, he was accepted in the school when someone else dropped out. He was overjoyed.

The ancestor of this institution, which was to be of lasting value to naturalists throughout the country, had been started by Mr. and Mrs. C. M. Goethe of Sacramento. They were wealthy philanthropists who studied educational systems and cultures as they traveled around the world. They had been especially charmed with the way in which some Europeans, notably the Danes, included outdoor nature study in their school curricula.

When they returned to California, the Goethes financed a European-type nature guide program at Lake Tahoe for the University of California. It was administrated by Dr. Harold C. Bryant and Carl's professor, Dr. Miller. The program was so popular that Stephen Mather, Director of the National Park Service, persuaded Bryant and Miller to move their school to Yosemite. By 1925, in addition to the offerings for the general public, they added the Yosemite School of Field Natural History. The Field School, as it was called, started the naturalist or interpretive services which have since spread throughout the national park system. Although it trained professional naturalists for the Park Service, the school was open to anyone who could show a good background in nature study. Many dedicated amateurs are counted among its graduates.

Dr. Bryant, a fine scholar and rather stern professor, was an impassioned crusader for the cause of conservation and wilderness. He wanted everyone to get to know nature first hand, and, as James Dewey was advocating in the field of education, to learn by doing. Bryant saw that to make converts to his cause he must take people into the mountains, must allow them to see the natural world in all its facets and moods and to confront it wholly. There could have been no more congenial viewpoint to Carl, who had been doing exactly that with his Trailfinders.

Each summer the Field School convened in Yosemite Valley for five weeks,

Carl, about 1930.

and moved for a final week to Tuolumne Meadows and the Yosemite back country. In the valley, the twenty students and their instructors stayed in Camp Nineteen near the Old Village or in the old Sentinel Hotel. Though the school and campground were free, students provided their own food and equipment.

Every morning they met outdoors or in the museum for a lecture and discussion period, and then walked out to see features which illustrated the lecture. Their excursions ranged as far as the Mariposa Grove of Big Trees and El Portal.

The five weeks in Yosemite Valley were divided into different subject areas led by specialists in botany, geology, forestry, mineralogy, insects, and wildlife. Climbing the rough talus slopes which foot the valley walls, the students examined their accumulated stones and discovered how many different kinds of granite form these seemingly uniform ramparts. Although Yosemite has no fossils, Dr. Ralph Chaney, a well-known paleobotanist, showed them metamorphic pebbles in the watercourses and explained that a lazy geologist doesn't need to climb mountains to find out what they're made of; he just waits for the streams to wash the rocks down to him. Later Carl studied with Dr. Chaney at Berkeley.

François Matthes, who had recently published his landmark *Geologic History of Yosemite*, frequently turned up for geology lectures and answered questions. Dr. Bryant was always present. It was a distinguished faculty.

Both a laboratory and a research library were available to the students, who were each required to submit a paper on some aspect of natural history. Carl decided to investigate the *Tintenstriche* or black streaks coursing down the granite walls of the valley. He discovered they are formed of a mixture of lichens and free-floating algae adhering to the stone along water-seeps. *Tintenstriche* is Afrikaans for similar streaks on granite bosses in South Africa. The word, which means ink streaks, amused Carl, evoking the old story of how Martin Luther threw a bottle of ink at the devil who was tempting him, and left a stain on the wall.

The Field School students and faculty had campfires every evening. One night, a big potluck dinner was laid out on flimsy camp tables. Carl, still shy, was thrown into messy confusion when a table suddenly upset and all the food went into his lap.

For the sixth week of the session the entire group hiked Yosemite's High Sierra loop trail and stayed — all except Carl — at the High Sierra Camps. Carl, who felt he couldn't afford the two dollars a night for luxury, back-packed and cooked his own food.

The group got up at five o'clock one morning to climb Mount Dana by hiking all the way from Tuolumne Meadows and ascending through the valley between Mounts Dana and Gibbs. Each person carried a bit of wood and some water to the top in order to make tea. Stumbling around among the summit rocks, Carl kicked over the water bucket. That was the end of the tea. The proper Dr. Bryant was visibly annoyed, and Carl could have wept from mortification.

It was a minor mishap, after all. Carl's wealth of experience, his thirst for knowledge, and his gift for working with people had become evident, and about halfway through the field school session he was asked to join the National Park Service staff as a ranger-naturalist for the following year. He always felt pride and pleasure at being the only one of the students thus singled out. Carl thereby became one of the earliest ranger-naturalists in the country, and could count among his teachers Dr. Bryant and Dr. Miller, who started it all.

Happy as he was, he had little inkling of the decisive step he had taken. It was the end of the quest, the beginning of a new life.

Branches

Helen as a high school girl.

13
Helen

By the spring of 1931, Carl was close to finishing college and already thinking about graduate school. And there was something else on his mind — pretty red-haired, freckle-faced Helen Katherine Myers whom he had met at the 1930 Yosemite Field School.

Helen, born in Oakland in 1905, was two years younger than Carl. Her mother died in 1926 when Helen was twenty-one, and three years later her father also passed away. At the University of California in Berkeley, Helen was an excellent student and a member of Lambda Omega sorority. A sociable person, she enjoyed many outdoor trips with her brother and her friends. In 1925 she backpacked with two other women in the Yosemite High Sierra she would come to think of as her own. She received the A.B. degree with a major in Zoology in 1927 and was elected to Phi Beta Kappa. A year later she had a Master's degree in zoology and a teaching credential and was elected to Sigma Xi, the honorary science fraternity.

In the fall of 1928, Helen bought a new Model A Ford Coupe and drove to Susanville for her first job, teaching biology in Lassen Union High School and Junior College. She was a popular teacher, distinguished by her quiet efficiency and her capacity to engage the imaginations of her students.

Helen was very close to her brother Ernest, who worked for a while as a ranger and was married in Yosemite. Later he became a doctor and orthopedic specialist at the Presidio in San Francisco. When Carl first met Helen, she was sharing a home with her brother.

Carl and Helen were immediately attracted to each other. He called her Jimmy, a nickname given by Ernest. Carl appreciated her fine mind and spirit, her love of the outdoors, and her sense of humor. Though slight of build, she was a strong hiker. It seemed that at last he had found a companion for his chosen way of life.

Helen was shy, but Carl wrote to her persistently during the following winter. At Christmas time they made a memorable trip to Death Valley together,

Helen during her teaching days at Susanville, 1930.

presaging many future trips. While it stormed and snowed, they huddled in the shelter at Dante's View eating broiled steaks. They were running out of water, so Carl drained the car radiator for dishwater. Driving the next day through a blinding snowstorm, he braked and got out to see where they were. He had strayed onto an unused older road, and miraculously had stopped right at the edge of a twenty foot dropoff where the mist was thickest.

When the summer of 1931 arrived and Carl returned to Tuolumne as a ranger-naturalist, Helen drove up in her little Model A to see him. On August 24th they were off to Reno to get married, celebrating their wedding supper in a restaurant in Bridgeport.

Then back to the meadows for a honeymoon in a wreck of a cabin oily from drums stored by the mosquito control team. The interior was painted battleship gray, and the rickety bed had broken-down springs and a mattress filled with corn shucks. The stove was about to collapse. The newlyweds carried water from an outside faucet and had only a candle until they got a Coleman lantern. On Saturdays a five gallon tin on the back of the wood stove heated bathwater for their galvanized iron washtub. They were gloriously happy.

Theirs was a public life; they could never tell who might pop in, or when. One pitch-black night Helen was leaning over the sink washing dishes by candlelight when they heard a banging at the door. Before they could answer, a strange figure blustered in. He reminded Carl of Robert W. Service's "The Shooting of Dan McGrew": a man "With a face most hair and the dreary stare of a dog whose day is done."

He ignored Carl, strode over to Helen, and held the tip of his big bowie knife right under her nose, pointing at some gleaming bits of yellow in his fist. "Looka this here," he growled as she shrank back in fear. "Lookit it! Lookit it!" He was harmless. He only wanted the rocks identified. They were iron pyrites — fool's gold.

That fall Helen gave up her job and they moved to a little apartment near the University of California at Los Angeles so that Carl could start graduate study. On his summer salary of eleven hundred dollars plus some of her savings, they managed to survive. Helen also went back to school to study plant anatomy with Dr. Flora Murray Scott. Dr. Scott, who was fresh from Scotland, paced up and down in a tartan as she lectured. Soon she and Helen were doing research together and co-authored several papers.

The botany department had a number of outstanding members: Dr.

Epling, a specialist in the mint family; Dr. Sponsler, engaged in advanced
studies of the structure of cellulose; and Dr. Haupt, who had been a student
of the famous Professor Chamberlain of Chicago, one of the foremost
authorities on cycads. Helen was becoming more and more fascinated with
plants, sharing Carl's enthusiasm as the two of them prepared for future graduate work.

Now that they had a home, they indulged their love of fine music by buying a phonograph and beginning a record collection. Carl's father gave them
his old Dodge. Since Helen had her Model A and they reckoned they didn't
need two cars, they sold the Dodge and bought an Underwood portable
typewriter with some of the money.

Each summer they returned to Yosemite where Carl had been assigned to
Tuolumne Meadows, Muir's sacred place of introduction to the High Sierra.
They found Yosemite Valley inspiring, but the high meadows and the timber-
line country above were heaven itself.

This greatest meadow of the Sierra Nevada stretches out like a pastoral
lawn in its shallow bowl. In early summer it is pale with dry grasses and
sedges. As the season proceeds it greens and livens with a wealth of flowers,
then dries again to autumn gold. Here and there bosses of glacial polish
gleam in the sun. The Tuolumne River meanders through, changeable and
yet serene. Around the open meadows stand forests of lodgepole pine with
their own store of botanical treasures. And above it all in jagged romantic display are glacier-rounded granite domes and glacier-plucked horn peaks
embellished by snowbanks and a truly alpine flora.

This enchanting upland would become Carl and Helen's second home.

14
Guardian of the Mountains

"You never enjoyed the world aright, till you so love the beauty of enjoying it,
that you are covetous and earnest to persuade others to enjoy it."
— Thomas Traherne

The summers in Tuolumne Meadows were wonderful to Carl and Helen. He felt he had found his true calling — to protect and expound the beauties of the Sierra. He knew that it would take dedication for the naturalist program to succeed, and believed that the future of the park depended in some measure upon his efforts. For it was largely through the naturalist program that the park could gain a loyal constituency. No missionary was ever more fiery than Carl as he set out to convert the heathen park visitors to his religion of the mountains.

In those days the Tuolumne campground was not delimited. People set-tled along both banks of the river and back into the woods. Many families established spots which they considered their own and to which they returned year after year. As long as their numbers were few, the park administration saw no harm in this casual arrangement.

Each morning Carl mounted his horse and rode out to meet the campers. He received warm and cheery greetings on every side, and was often invited to stop for a cup of coffee or some delicious new concoction created over an open fire.

The rest of the day he would lead a hike or climb. The Pied Piper of Tuolumne, he soon had a large following wherever he went. He was free to work out his own schedule, and by varying his destinations he managed to explore all the nooks and crannies, peaks and valleys around the meadows.

When evening came, Carl would conduct a campfire, telling stories, lead-ing songs (many of them learned with the Trailfinders), and preaching his gospel of wilderness. Late each night he returned exhausted to his tent. Yet he and Helen often stayed up even later by candlelight typing reports and trip schedules to post about the campground.

The reports he turned in at the end of each season show prodigious work. For example, in August, 1931 he spent fifteen days as follows:

Saturday, arranged flowers for flower display, made out schedules for week; left 10 A.M. for Mount Lyell with a party.

Sunday, climbed Lyell and Maclure.

Monday, returned from Lyell, arriving at Tuolumne Meadows 11:30 A.M.; afternoon flower walk; evening campfire.

Tuesday, all day trip to Mt. Conness; evening campfire.

Wednesday, (rainy morning) worked on schedules and field notes; afternoon, Lembert Dome; evening campfire with 250 people.

Thursday, all day trip up Mt. Dana; evening campfire.

Friday, all day trip to Glen Aulin; evening campfire.

Saturday, arranged flower exhibit; afternoon nature walk; evening campfire.

Sunday, pressed plants, worked on field notes and official correspondence.

Monday, all day trip to Budd Lake and up Echo Peaks.

Tuesday, all day trip to Gaylor Lakes; evening campfire.

Wednesday, museum in morning, Lembert Dome in afternoon, evening campfire.

Thursday, all day to Mt. Dana; evening campfire.

Friday, cancelled Parker Pass trip to hunt for lost man on Conness Glacier all day.

Saturday, Summit Mt. Conness.

No, there weren't any days off. On August 10, 1933, he returned from an overnight trip to Waterwheel Falls by 7:30 A.M., and that day took 41 people up Mount Dana. That summer he took one and a half days off during the season. Gradually he slid in a free Sunday here and there, and by 1946 he was up to two days off a week, Tuesday and Friday. This was deceptive, however, for he generally used free days for naturalist work. He might drive to the Valley to meet with officials, or hike with the Field School, or accompany visiting dignitaries on a tour of the area. Sometimes he led an artist or biologist to some choice spot, or spent the day collecting seeds of alpine plants for a foreign botanist. Or he might be off exploring the peaks, sometimes with Helen and sometimes alone.

Carl was in his element, but he pressed himself so hard that often Helen had to do his writing for him. She helped him in other ways, too.

Conness glacier party, 1932. NPS Photo.

Occasionally he was called away to search for a missing person and she would conduct a hike in his absence, reporting as Helen K. Sharsmith, H. R. N. W. P. (Honorary Ranger Naturalist Without Pay). She answered questions at the flower display, and once in a while gave an evening campfire. Despite her involvement, at times she must have felt Carl had forgotten about her in his devotion to his work.

At first there was something of a feud between the regular rangers and the naturalists, called "butterfly chasers" and "posy pickers." The rangers could make Carl's life rather miserable. Once he built a stand of two by fours and haywire with a display of fresh wildflowers in discarded ginger ale bottles. While he was away on a hike, the temporary "regulars" used the bottles for target practice, and he returned at the end of the day to find his display in ruins.

When the Field School had its last week in the High Country each summer, Carl was invited to go along as guide and naturalist. In this way he met many eminent scientists who came to the school.

Among the most memorable were the Cloos brothers, Hans and Ernst. In

Carl in his ranger uniform with Jimmy Car, 1937.

the mountains along the German-Czech border, they had hit upon the theory of the pluton or batholith — a huge subterranean upwelling of granite
which forms a mountain range. Ernst, a tall, vigorous man, had come to
study the extent of the Sierra batholith, tracing the shear where the granite
meets the metamorphic rocks as indicated by dark streaks in the granite. Carl
learned much from him.

One year, Hans Cloos hiked in to Evelyn Lake to meet the Field School.
He reported to Carl that he had been startled to see a young couple up there
toasting frogs on sticks over a fire. It seems they had made a bet they could
live off the back country. Whoever chickened out first had to buy the other as
much ice cream as he could eat when they returned to the valley. Cloos had
heard Americans were crazy and he now had the evidence. Evidence, too, of
how hard it was and is for park rangers to protect the delicate alpine creatures.

One summer day, Carl agreed to pick up the Cloos brothers on their way
back from Mount Dana. He forgot. When in late afternoon he suddenly
remembered his appointment, he hurried to Tioga Pass in his car. As the
brothers approached they were singing, "*Es gibt doch keine* Carl Sharsmith,
Carl Sharsmith, Carl Sharsmith" (There isn't any Carl Sharsmith). Later Hans
wrote a book, *Conversation with the Earth*, which Carl greatly admired. To
Cloos the earth was a living thing full of dynamic forces forever active — a
view that has become ever more accepted.

Enid Michael was a self-taught Yosemite botanist with eyes like blue ice
and an unyielding spirit to match. She intimidated Carl and many others. If
he inadvertently stepped on a flower in Enid's presence, he got a good scolding. Her husband Charlie was a well-known climber (Michael's Minaret is
named for him), and together they scrambled up many high places and sometimes found rare flowers. Enid had the annoying habit, however, of inventing
names for the localities where the plants had been found, so no one else could
check her information.

Geologist François Matthes was a great favorite, and Carl treasured the
times they spent in the field together. Matthes was a gentle and genial
European who had made the Sierra his vocation. He often used to say, "If
those rocks could speak, what an interesting story they would tell!" He
showed Carl the curious deep depressions on Pothole Dome. They were pot-
holes that had been formed, Matthes said, by glacial meltwater plunging from
above down a crevasse in the glacier.

Once Carl and Matthes went up the Sunrise Trail from Little Yosemite and
climbed Moraine Dome, which Matthes had named. As they ascended, the

geologist pointed out that they were passing a succession of moraines, the lower ones the most recently formed. He hit the rocks of the first moraine with his hammer and they rang like a bell. Higher up they gave a dull thud. On top, the rocks of the very oldest moraine fell apart when he struck them.

A short distance from the top is a semicircular moraine. When they finally stood on the summit they could see an aplite dike once level with the surface, now weathered out like a wall. Near the dike is a great erratic block studded with huge crystals, carried by the glaciers all the way from the Tuolumne Meadows area hundreds of thousands of years ago.

Matthes instituted the measurement of the glaciers each year in order to plot their movements and recession. In the fall of 1933, Ranger Naturalist Bert Harwell was out measuring on Lyell Glacier when he discovered the corpse of a mountain sheep lying on the surface. At first he thought it was alive, it was so little deteriorated. He and his companion tasted the meat; it reminded them of jerky. A German geologist who was in the Yosemite Museum at the time asked for some tallow to send to his laboratory in Germany. Later he wrote an article revealing that the tallow was in a state of transition to petroleum. The animal had probably fallen into a crevasse about sixty years before and had been preserved in a cold moist environment until it finally melted out. Carl became involved when he studied the sheep's stomach contents and ascertained from the seeds that its last meal was eaten on the east side of the Sierra.

Another distinguished naturalist, Joe Dixon, became director of instruction in the Field School in the summer of 1933. He was an authority on Alaskan wildlife, and also knew Yosemite intimately. In 1915 he had worked with Grinnell and Storer on field research which led to the publication of their landmark book *Animal Life of the Yosemite*. Dixon had co-authored several other books with Dr. Grinnell and Dr. Jean M. Linsdale, notably *Fur Bearing Mammals of California*.

Once in a while around a campfire Dixon talked of his past, of his acquaintance with the great arctic explorer Stefansson, and of an iced-in winter he spent in the Canadian arctic. He persuaded the Field School to break away from the High Sierra Camps and take off-trail excursions to many little-known corners of the park. In Dixon, Carl found a new mentor in the ways of the wilderness.

Helen was a strong, creative woman who threw herself into life in Tuolumne Meadows with enthusiasm. She worked hard, hiked hard, learned everything she could about the natural scene, and made many friends. Soon she was writing articles for Yosemite Nature Notes describing her observations and her thoughts.

In 1935 she gave an exuberant account of a strenuous backpack with her friend Jane McIntire up Yosemite Falls to the head of Yosemite Creek, into Ten Lakes Basin, up the canyon of the South Fork of Cathedral Creek to the top of Tuolumne Peak, on to May and Tenaya Lakes, and returning to Yosemite Valley by the Tenaya Zigzags. In those days it was very unusual for women to backpack without the company of men. Helen was not a rebel; she simply did it because she enjoyed it. When Carl was occupied leading groups, she hiked with her friends, and later with her children.

She took up photography, too, and made a photographic record of these years. It became a lifetime hobby. On a memorable morning in 1936, at the end of a photography course in Yosemite Valley, she started walking to Tuolumne Meadows. It was a lovely summer day and she decided to go by way of Merced Lake. She reached the meadows at seven P.M., having hiked thirty-three miles and climbed six thousand feet. The following week she went back to the Valley to develop her film. This time she hiked up the short way, only twenty-two miles.

She started a series of journals devoted, not to the humdrum details of life, but to the trips she took with and without Carl — a record of the good times. In small, neat bound books she chronicled weekends and longer trips from 1933 until 1972, when illness made her unable to write any longer.

Carl's parents, who were delighted with Helen and pleased that he was progressing in his chosen field, began to go camping. The impetus came from Marie, who bought knickers and high-topped boots, a Coleman lantern, and a tent. They even (Mama eager and Papa dragging) visited Carl and Helen in Tuolumne Meadows.

In the fall of 1932, Carl and Helen transferred to the University of California at Berkeley, and the following spring he received his Bachelor's degree in botany from the University of California at Los Angeles. By the next fall, 1933, both of them were working for their doctorates in botany.

15
Berkeley & the Arctic-Alpine Flora

Berkeley was to be the culmination of a long pilgrimage. As Tuolumne Meadows had become the center of Carl's outdoor life, so Berkeley became the center, the intellectual hub he had been approaching elliptically but with fierce determination for so many years. The training he received there would remain as a standard of precision and dedication his whole life long.

He had become interested in the ecological theories of Dr. Henry Cowles of the Univerisity of Chicago. Although similar studies were well advanced in Europe, Cowles was among the few American advocates of this branch of biology at the time. Carl hoped to study ecology. With this purpose in mind, soon after he arrived in Berkeley Carl went to see William Albert Setchell, head of the botany department. He was a deeply learned man, an authority on marine algae, ferns, and climatic plant distribution, who sometimes wrote on his blackboard in Greek and Latin. In his deep dignified voice, Dr. Setchell asked, "What are you interested in?"

"Botany."

"What kind of botany?"

"Well, I thought I would like to get more deeply into ecology."

Dr. Setchell laughed at this mention of what he considered a kind of dilettante natural history. "I don't know about ecology," he said, "but we can teach you something about plants."

Although Carl was disappointed in not being able to pursue his initial interest, he took every course Dr. Setchell offered. By the time he graduated, Carl had joined Setchell's little coterie of students who explored San Francisco French restaurants with the portly and pleasure-loving professor, and were allowed to call him "Uncle Bill." Setchell's familiarity with favored and promising students led to the erroneous impression that he had a nepotistic circle of relatives on campus.

Carl often looked back on his Berkeley days with profound appreciation of his professors, most of whom were famous old-timers near the end of their careers. In addition to Setchell and Willis Linn Jepson, Carl studied with the geneticist Ernest B. Babcock and the paleobotanist Ralph W. Chaney.

The *enfant terrible* of the department was Professor Jepson. He had written the *Manual of the Flowering Plants of California* in 1923, and was revered by all incoming students. Reverence changed to fear and trembling when they discovered that the great man was fierce and implacable, jealous of his power and position, and stingy with his time for students unless they were women.

Although Jepson seemed oblivious, his students found it politic to be seen working busily in the anteroom outside his office every morning at nine. Each day, Carl was there perched on a high stool and hunched over his botanical work. He would hear the hall door open and the squeak, squeak of Jepson's shoes as he crossed the room, entered his spacious office and shut the door, not to be seen for the rest of the day.

In one of Jepson's seminars Carl was assigned a difficult and controversial paper by a British botanist named Saunders. When he gave his report, he struggled to clarify the points in the paper. Finally he blurted, "I wish Miss Saunders had written the darn thing so one could understand it better."

Some days later as Carl sat at his usual station, the squeaky shoes stopped just behind his stool, and there was a portentous clearing of the throat. A rusty voice said, "Mr. Sharsmith!"

Carl jumped to his feet and faced the overpowering Dr. Jepson. "Mr. Sharsmith," he growled, "in my forty years' roster of graduate students, you are the first to have used profanity in my presence!" Carl could only cringe as Jepson launched into a lengthy and wonderful discourse on the adequacy, the expressiveness, and the wealth of the English language, which has no need of expletives for emphasis. It was a lecture he never forgot.

Carl began preparing his thesis under Dr. Jepson. But since Jepson was on the point of retirement, Carl realized he would have to change advisors. He had a high opinion of Dr. Herbert Mason, whom he had known in the Field School, so he explained the dilemma to him.

"I will be glad to work with you," Mason said, "but it must be cleared with the Department Chairman, Dr. Hoaglund."

"I believe we can settle this easily enough," Dr. Hoaglund told Carl. "I'll just drop across the hall and see Dr. Jepson. You can wait here." He was gone for quite some time. Eventually Hoaglund burst through the door, flung himself into a chair, and mopped his perspiring brow. Suddenly noticing Carl, he shouted, "Get out!" Apparently, though Jepson had shown little interest in Carl's thesis, he felt a student was being stolen from him — and to add insult to injury, the thief was Mason, his arch-enemy in some arcane academic squabble.

Both Carl and Helen studied with Dr. Mason, and Carl became his teaching assistant in taxonomy, finally completing his thesis under Mason's supervision. Mason, a specialist in the paleobotany of the closed-cone pines, had done research with Dr. Chaney, also a Field School instructor. Helen, too, worked in the department. At various times she was head teaching assistant in General Botany, a teaching assistant in Systematic Botany, and a botanical researcher for Jepson. The money she brought in helped to keep them solvent.

Early in his career at Berkeley, Carl received word that President Gordon Sproul wished to see him. He reported to the president's office in great trepidation, wondering what he could possibly have done.

When Sproul entered, he addressed Carl by his first name and began chatting about his courses, how he had become interested in botany, and so on. Realizing these were preliminaries, Carl waited in dread.

Finally Sproul remarked, "I see you are not a dilettante." (Carl looked up the word as soon as he had left the office.) At last he came to the point. "Carl, I have a son named Bobby. He's just about eleven years old, and I don't know how to talk to him about certain things. I want you to take him out somewhere and teach him about how life begins."

So Carl and Bobby went up Strawberry Canyon, and Carl told the boy about the birds and the bees.

Carl knew that he wanted to do his thesis on the alpine flora of the Sierra Nevada, and began reading widely about alpine botany. Little had been written about the plants of the High Sierra, aside from Smiley's 1921 *Report upon the Boreal Flora of the Sierra Nevada of California*. Smiley's was the most complete listing available at the time. And Harvey M. Hall, whom Carl had met in the Field School in 1931, and for whom the Hall Natural Area is named, had discovered a few new plants in the Tuolumne Meadows region.

It was not going to be easy. Beside the paucity of information, there was little interest at Berkeley in Carl's chosen subject. Already, laboratory studies of tissues and physiological processes on a microscopic level were more highly regarded than the rather old-fashioned field work which Carl aspired to. Ecological studies were as yet only in their beginnings.

Through his reading of European sources, Carl realized that much had been and was being done to clarify the distribution and history of arctic-alpine

Dr. Herbert Mason, 1938. Photo by Russell   *Dr. William Setchell, 1936.*
S. Miller courtesy of the NPS.

floras. He struggled through volumes in French and German, even Russian and Norwegian with some help from his friends.

There was a study center for arctic-alpine flora at the University of Colorado. There Dr. Theodore Holm, who had earlier worked in Greenland, had studied the alpine plants of the Rockies, and the university contained his extensive collection. Carl knew of the center, but it never occurred to him to go to Colorado for his degree. The Sierra was his range, and so it would remain. Although it had fewer species than the Rockies, there were fewer scholars studying them and some big ideas to deal with. He was content.

He realized that the flora of the Sierra Nevada is not a single isolated flora. It is connected to the whole world in its own peculiar fashion. It shares many plant families with other mountain ranges, and other families which one would expect to find in the Sierra are unaccountably absent. These distributions surely represent the accidents of history acting upon the nature of the plants themselves.

First, history. This globe has sitting on its head a circumpolar icecap — what is left of the vast ice sheets which flowed down across North America, Europe, and Asia in glacial times. As the climate warmed and the ice sheets slowly retreated, the plants associated with them — plants that could stand cold dry winds and freezing temperatures — retreated too. They left the valleys which had become too warm and moist for them, and migrated to inhospitable fell-fields, the chill shadow of rocky ledges, and the borders of icy streams.

As landscape and climate changed, so did the plants. With the passage of time, the species that survived evolved subtle physiological adaptations to high elevations which their low-altitude arctic forms had not achieved. Thus the so-called arctic-alpine flora shows a range of fascinating relationships and subtle differences.

There was more. Why aren't the floras on all mountain ranges even more similar? If the centers from which they spread were contiguous lowland areas, shouldn't all the mountain ranges near these areas inherit equally their retreating flora?

Carl learned that the Norwegians and others, observing still-glaciated areas in Greenland, Canada, and northern Europe, noticed certain elevated terrains which, owing to accidents of situation, remained unglaciated even though surrounded by miles of ice. They named these "nunataks" from an Inuit word for a hill surrounded by lower terrain. Nunataks are by their very nature *refugia,* or places of refuge for cold-weather plants which have disappeared from surrounding lowlands. Investigators theorized that when the ice finally retreated, the melted-off areas surrounding the nunataks were colonized by warmer-weather plant groups from farther south, leaving the cold-weather plants on the nunataks isolated from their arctic relatives by perhaps thousands of miles.

Carl was excited by the nunatak theory, and wondered if it were applicable to the Sierra Nevada. Certainly some species occur there in comparative isolation, and other plants, such as the *Dryas* found in the Alps and the Canadian and American Rockies, are missing.

As he delved deeper, he knew that in order to form a coherent picture of the history and distribution of Sierran plants, he would have to know much more about them. He would, in effect, have to describe the flora more completely than had ever been done. This would mean exploring more widely the upper reaches of his "delectable mountains."

16
The Sierran Alpine Expedition

*"... as if into these mountain mansions Nature had taken pains to
gather her choicest treasures to draw her lovers into close and confiding
communion with her."*
— John Muir

In the summer of 1937, Carl arranged with the Park Service to work in
Yosemite Valley during June while it was still too early to collect in the
High Sierra, and to be replaced by another man for the second half of
the summer. When July came, Carl and Helen borrowed Marie's tent
and Coleman lantern and set out with their plant presses in the little car.

They would drive up a roadhead as far into the mountains as they could,
then hike or backpack, collecting as they moved. Sometimes they made a high
camp, staggering in with their loot at the end of a long collecting day almost
too tired to tackle camp chores. Many a day the plant presses were two or
three feet thick with specimens. Back at the roadhead they had to dry their
finds and write up hastily taken notes by lantern light, often not getting into
their sleeping bags until midnight.

One of the most delightful of Helen's journals describes this "Sierran
Alpine Expedition." They started from Tioga Pass and camped July 11 at
Tioga Lake. It proved so windy they had to retreat to a more sheltered spot
nearby. Several days were spent exploring Dana Plateau, Mount Gibbs, and
Mount Lewis, and taking a four day backpack to Kuna Crest. "It is very beau-
tiful and peaceful and we are very content."

On July 23 they climbed Lee Vining Peak, traversed a long ridge, and
went to the top of Mount Warren. As they descended, night was falling. "Oh,
Carl," said Helen, "Let's bivouac. That's something I've always wanted to
do." He thought it a splendid idea. They found a close-matted cluster of
whitebark pines and built a small warm fire. Drawing piles of pine duff
around them, they split their last sandwich, curled up, and went to sleep, wak-
ing at hourly intervals to replenish the fire and gaze up at a golden half moon.

As Somerset Maugham wrote of another place and time, this was romance!

The next day they started driving north on Highway 395, but fifty miles up the road Carl realized he had left his shovel at Tioga Lake. In complete silence they drove back. The shovel was waiting at the lake, and they both laughed with relief and started speaking again. Returning north, they sentimentally drove the length of Bridgeport twice in order to pass the restaurant where they had celebrated their wedding supper six years before. When they reached Leavitt Meadows they had time to climb Leavitt Peak. Coming back late to camp, Helen asked, "What reward do I get for all this hard work?"

"Love and kisses," Carl replied.

At Virginia Lakes, Carl got the fire going and biscuits browning in the reflector oven. The next day they climbed Dunderberg Peak. "8 P.M. and a fine dinner of cabbage, hamhocks and biscuits...At 10 we are through with work on plants and sit drowsily by the fire." The next day Helen noted, "we have a stack of wet plants in presses and all the blotters we have with us must be dried." After completing that job, they headed south again to explore the area around the Devil's Postpile, climb Mammoth Mountain, and visit Convict Lake. Driving on to Rock Creek Basin, they made a base camp late in the day. She washed their clothes by dark.

Morning...Carl mended Helen's shoes before taking off to climb part way up Mount Morrison, while she stayed in camp to develop film, wash clothes, pack for the morrow's backpack, and make plum duff for dinner. Carl returned at 8. "I'm so glad he is back; it was getting lonesome. He found a new *Draba* which seems very interesting."

Up at 6, and work on plants until 11:30 AM, when they prepared for another backcountry jaunt. Their packs weighed in at 35 and 45 pounds. To save weight, "we are trying it with only one sleeping bag." Over Mono Pass they reached a spot high above an alpine lake for camp. "We leisurely cook and eat our dinner, then bask in the warmth of our campfire, Carl tugging at his pipe, I writing this account. Stars glisten overhead, the music of falling water sings out merrily, campfire lights play upon the white-bark pines; all else is silent and dark."

The next day they climbed Mount Mills, lunching on raspberry ice cream of snow, sugar, and kool-aid. Returning to camp they packed up for an after-dinner departure. "We had fruit for breakfast and dinner soaking..Carl carries the billy-can of fruit in his hand...a half-hour climb up to the pass...By the time we begin the descent it is dark. There is no moon but the whiteness of the granite and the reflected light from a sky full of stars give us something more than total darkness…It is a very bad trail. Carl says it was never properly built but just seems to have chewed its way into the mountainside from long use…It goes up and down without reason and is full of holes and boulders…I spill several times…Looking down on Ruby Lake we see a silver plume of light upon the water. We wonder, for there is no moon. We look up and realize that it is Jupiter's reflected light reflected once again in the waters far below us. We are in harmony with the night and mountains around us. We feel a part of them…We rest awhile, and laughingly refresh ourselves from the pot of fruit Carl still clutches. But we talk in whispers not to disturb the silence of the night. We reach camp at 10 P.M. We are warm but not hot. Carl feels the waters of Rock Creek as we cross them to our tent. 'Come on, Jimmy,' he says, 'strip.' Inwardly protesting I obey, and in the darkness we go naked down to the stream and soap ourselves and wash in the cold waters. I think it a somewhat heroic deed but back in the tent, our neighbors quite unaware of what went on, I am glowingly warm."

In Bishop they gorged on ice cream before driving to North Lake and packing over Paiute Pass to Humphreys Basin. There Carl recalled his earlier trip with the Trailfinders. Poking around the slope among the stunted white-bark pines he found a tiny rock fireplace, the heart of his old camp. A rusted can labeled Lyle's Golden Syrup remained as a memento. He also discovered where he had cut off some whitebark twigs above his bed. "A branch is grown out just below the cut. He removes it and counts the rings — surely enough, seven of them, and counting the terminal bud scars gives seven again. I keep that twig for a remembrance."

They climbed up the surrounding slopes to collect plants. "It is all so love-ly," Helen wrote. "I can hardly comprehend my presence here. I know now why Carl says the Tuolumne region is a mere postage stamp to the Sierra as a whole. So it may be, but if it can be classified thus, it is a philatelist's prized rarity."

"Back at camp at 6:30, Carl makes dinner over the same little fireplace of seven years ago. The same fireplace, the same bed, the same Carl, the same lit-tle, black cooking pots, the same Stetson hat. But Jimmy is extra this time. Carl tells me, 'each article on a go-lite trip must pay in convenience and com-fort for the trouble of its transportation, and a substitute, though inferior, is better than the carrying of special contrivances.' I ask him if he is glad he brought me."

"We do not wake early this morning for we slept miserably the first part of last night. When the temperature is even a little above cold it is almost intoler-

able for the two of us to sleep so cramped up in a single bag." In a shallow
stream Carl caught a mess of golden trout in his hands for dinner. They felt
some misgivings about taking the lives of these beautiful creatures, but
hunger overcame their scruples.

Back on the road, they made a desert camp on their way to Onion Valley.
Dinner was cooked on sagebrush and cow patties. "Buffalo chips, by gosh,"
said Carl.

Hiking up to Kearsarge Pass they saw a rubber boat on a little lake. "Carl
has an almost uncontrollable desire to swim out and stick it with a pin." Later
when Helen set the camera time-release and took their picture together, he
"makes a terrible face as he gnaws and growls on his jerky, I am looking
pained and reproachful, trying to get him to cease the antics. The snap of the
shutter catches us thus." They climbed University Peak in a storm of rain and
hail. On the way down they picked ripe elderberries, and that evening they
boiled up some elderberry juice. Carl cut Helen's hair.

Hiking in from Whitney Portal, Carl and Helen climbed Whitney in hail,
rain and wind. "It is pretty cold, but we persist in our efforts for Carl is
finding long-sought plants." A windy night at Mirror Lake, as the fire blew in
their faces. Although it was near here that they discovered the one plant
named for them, *Hackelia sharsmithii*, Helen did not mention it in the journal. It was merely one of hundreds of specimens. The plant seemed unfamil-
iar, but only extended study would confirm it as a new, never-before-
described species. It is an attractive mountain forget-me-not with blue flowers
and rounded leaves, growing under large boulders in the area near Mirror
Lake.

In a camp above Carroll Creek on August 24th, they marked their sixth
wedding anniversary with canned chicken, peaches and cake. After dinner
Carl polished to perfection a rusted frying pan he had found in the dump at
Mirror Lake. The next day climbing Wonoga Peak, Helen wondered why she
was so full of absolute bliss. "He suggests that is perhaps because there are no
'goof' tourists on this trail to insert a jarring note into the picture. He is correct." They considered themselves the aristocrats of the mountains, and
looked down on non-backpackers. In those days they seldom met any of their
own kind.

Approaching a pass, they greeted a party with a mule. The people were
"sitting on their haunches...The woman, with an inimicable tone of consola-
tion and sympathy, responds 'Oh, do you really think you will be able to
make it?' A season's pent-up annoyance at these tourists gives way in me. 'I

am accustomed to,' I retort snappily, in rather nasty tone, and go on up the trail without losing my stride."

"This, the first day of our seventh year together, has been a completely happy one...it has taken time for the growth of mutual understanding and intimate companionship."

On the trail to the Siberian Plateau they found some tiny *Androsace*, members of the primrose family not previously known south of Yosemite. They made camp in a dry meadow, and Carl dug a spring. Helen noted that it was her thirty-second birthday. "A happy day it has been." In the morning Carl's spring was full of clear water.

North they went again over the Kingsbury Grade, where Helen

Ranger/Naturalist Carl Sharsmith, 1935. Photo by John Applegarth, courtesy of the NPS.

recalled driving to Susanville in her little new Ford on the way to start teaching in 1928. They climbed Freel Peak in a high wind. Back at Tioga Lake the wind was still blowing, and again they retreated to Slate Creek. Over the campfire, Carl sang German songs. "We are happy," Helen writes, "but it is happiness tinged with a poignant feeling. Tomorrow will be the last day of our alpine summer."

In this way they lived from late July through September, starting in Yosemite and working north, then south almost to the end of the range, and back north again. They were trying to sample every region in the Sierra Nevada above tree line, from as far south as Mount Whitney and the northern margin of the Kern Plateau, to the last outpost of timberline near Lake Tahoe.

In addition to the *Hackelia*, there were, over time, other discoveries. On the Dana Plateau, Carl found a minute white flower which turned out to be *Cerastium beringianum*, previously described as a western arctic from both sides of the Bering Sea. Yet there was reason to expect to find it, for in the herbarium at Berkeley Carl had discovered it along with two other plants collected in the High Sierra by La Bouchère many years before. No one else had located these three, and Jepson must have assumed their presence among the Sierra specimens stemmed from a labeling error.

A second find was *Gentiana tenella*, Dane's gentian, the only gentian we have in common with Europe, and possibly the only dicot we have in common with the Alps. It too was on the Dana Plateau, a Sierran nunatak, as well as at the base of Mount Muir in the southern Sierra.

The third of La Bouchère's plants was a snow willow, *Salix nivalis*. Carl had searched and searched, but it eluded him. In 1933 Carlton Ball, greatest American specialist on willows, came to Tuolumne Meadows with his friend Vernon Bailey, an eminent mammalogist who had been on the Death Valley Scientific Expedition of 1893. These two set to work to find the snow willow.

One evening in that year Carl was invited to Parsons Lodge in Tuolumne Meadows for a campfire. As the group assembled, he saw Dr. Ball come running from one side, and Dr. Bailey from the other, each triumphantly waving a tiny sample of the coveted willow. Dr. Ball had found his specimen in Glacier Canyon by Mount Dana, and Bailey's was from Koip Peak Pass.

On the 1937 expedition, Carl and Helen several times mailed huge packets of specimens back to Berkeley for later study. When at last they had their specimens and notes in good shape, they turned the entire collection over to the University of California Herbarium, the most comprehensive collection of alpine Sierran flora ever made.

Meanwhile Helen had been working on her own thesis — a flora of the Mount Hamilton Range. During the school year she collected the material on day or weekend trips, occasionally accompanied by Carl or her friend Annetta Carter, but more often alone. In the brief blooming season before the onslaught of summer heat she climbed up and down this hilly country, made little camps in secluded spots, and amassed a considerable collection and voluminous notes. Although the effort was less innovative than Carl's in the Sierra, it was a landmark flora. It was published in 1945 and a revised edition remains in print.

Both Carl and Helen had passed their qualifying exams and were ready to start on the flora of the Sierra Nevada when a new development occurred. Carl was offered a job.

17
Hills of the Palouse

C arl never intended to become a college professor. He was a
dreamer pursuing knowledge for its own sake and letting the
future take care of itself. Furthermore, he and Helen were determined to finish their doctorates. However, in 1937 when he was
offered a teaching position at Washington State College in Pullman, the economy was still in depression. He and Helen were running short of money, and
jobs were few and far between. He accepted.

He assumed he would be able to complete his flora and thesis while on the
job. Meanwhile he would finally be supporting himself and Helen — though
in truth he had not worried too much about that. At Berkeley Helen had
worked at various times in the botany department, and in 1935 and 1936 she
was instructor in botany and bacteriology at Mills College. None of these
part-time positions paid much, but no matter how little money came in they
always seemed to manage. Only later did Carl realize that Helen must have
been digging into her savings to eke out their slender resources.

In the fall of 1937 they went to Pullman, located in a little hollow between
the hills of the rolling, almost treeless Palouse — a landscape formed of a dust
called loess which accumulated hundreds of thousands of years ago as wind-
blown deposits on the periphery of the great continental glaciers. Winters
were much colder in Pullman than at Berkeley, gray skies covered the spare
landscape, and at times the wind lashed harshly across the duncolored waves
of grasss. Carl and Helen felt isolated in a somber unlovely Siberia and longed
for California.

He was asked to teach the botanic section of a range management course.
Fortunately he had studied grasses with Jepson, but the course still required
intensive preparation, and he worked very hard.

In addition to teaching range ecology and taxonomy Carl was given
responsibility for the herbarium. All the early collections of some well-known
plant explorers were there. One of these was Wilhelm Suksdorf, a curious
German who had decided to find every plant that grew in Skamania County,

Washington, and did. Another, William C. Cusick, came west in the early days
and did his work in the Blue Mountains of Oregon. Taxonomists all over the
world were interested in these collections, and Carl found himself with a
worldwide correspondence. Helen found herself typing for him again, as well
as teaching a methods course for future botany instructors.

Every weekend they could get away they went exploring, driving into the
Blue Mountains of Oregon, down to Boise and Sun Valley, and northeast to
Mount Spokane. They camped and picnicked even when it was cold or
stormy and collected for the herbarium whenever possible. The trips afield
provided relief from their sense of confinement in Pullman.

At the time, the government was building the Grand Coulee Dam, and
Kettle Falls was soon to be inundated by the backed-up waters of the
Columbia River. Carl knew that David Douglas, an early plant explorer, had
collected in the region, and thus it was the type-locality for a number of well-
known plants. Hoping to find and identify the same species as are in the original Douglas collection in London's Kew Gardens, he and Helen organized a
camping trip to Kettle Falls with two of Carl's students. Although they made
a sizeable collection, he never found the time to work them over. They are
probably still waiting on their yellowed sheets in the old herbarium at
Pullman.

In those days the administration of the college was intensely puritanical.
Teachers were expected to live straight, think clean, and go to bed early.
When Carl served on the doctoral committee, the professors had to take their
smoking breaks by walking out of the building and down a nearby street.
One evening the botany department had a picnic in the hills. They roasted
wienies over a campfire and began a rollicking song-fest. At nine o'clock the
department chairman, a deacon of the church, came forward with a bucket of
water and announced curfew by dousing the fire.

A minor scandal developed when the dean discovered that one of the faculty members kept some wine in his house. The professor was called on the
carpet by the president. Shortly thereafter, the pianist Josef Hoffmann and his
wife came to Pullman to give a concert. At the reception afterwards, the
dean's wife asked Mrs. Hoffmann, "Is there something your husband would
like to drink?"

"Oh," was the reply, "a glass of wine would be nice." In consternation the
dean had to hunt up the erring professor to furnish the drinks.

On autumn evenings, Helen and Carl went to the classroom building to
mount plant specimens. He had a student named Jackie working for him on a

Hiking in the Wallowa Mountains of Oregon, 1938.

government Works Progress Administration grant, and she brought her boyfriend to help out. The heat was turned off about five in the afternoon, and as autumn progressed the building grew colder and colder. One day Jackie's boyfriend was hauled before the dean on the shocking accusation that he had been seen entering the building in the evening with a blanket.

As he corresponded with botanists in such far places as France and Rumania, Berlin and Moscow, Carl exchanged plant specimens and built up the Washington State College herbarium. In order to organize the exchanges, he built shelves with cubbyholes labeled with the names of twenty-two different institutions and gradually collected piles of plants to send to each. The professor whom Carl had replaced had a great excess of pressed *Eriophyllum*, and before leaving he suggested that Carl might give them away. They were duly distributed among the twenty-two cubbyholes.

One warm afternoon the head of the botany department strolled into the herbarium, leafed through the materials lying around, and strolled out without a word. Shortly afterwards Carl was summoned to the office of the president — a pompous gentleman who always drove up the college hill in low gear with one hand on the car horn, bowing to the students as he passed. "I hear," he accused, "that you have been giving away valuable plant materials from the herbarium." It took some explaining for the astonished Carl to set things right again.

Far worse than these petty annoyances was his growing sense of frustration at not having finished his thesis. He felt he must get back to Berkeley, its library and its herbarium. Each August he returned to the Yosemite Field School as an instructor, but his ten month contract at Pullman made it impossible for him to work the season as a ranger-naturalist in his beloved Tuolumne Meadows.

In late July and early August, 1938, Carl and the Field School went to the Tiltill Valley northeast of Hetch Hetchy, where they found lilies ten feet tall. While Carl was away, Helen and her friend Annetta Carter took an extended backpack from Glacier Point to the Clark Range, then south of the Ritter Range to Devil's Postpile, north along the Muir Trail to Shadow Creek, by side trail to Lake Ediza, by Garnet and Thousand Island Lakes, over Donohue Pass to Ireland Creek, then up to Ireland and Fletcher Lakes, over Vogelsang Pass to Little Yosemite, and down to Yosemite Valley. Much of the early part of the trip was cross-country in stormy conditions before the snow had melted. One night they sat cramped in a rock cave drying their sodden clothes by a tiny fire while the wind howled outside. Another night a pack rat ate holes in all their clothes.

After losing their route, wading knee deep through icy streams and plunging to their hips in snowdrifts, Helen wrote, "This has been an adventurous but dream-fulfilling day. For long I have wanted to go to Ottoway Lakes; for long I have wanted to work cross-country with pack, on my own responsibility; for long I have wanted to have my own timberline camp, far away from trail. All these I have had today." Apparently with Annetta she felt a type of freedom that she could not experience with Carl, who was more experienced, more knowledgeable, and perhaps a bit more like a parent.

Work with the Field School gave Carl some chance to continue his Sierra studies, and even to make discoveries. Near the McCabe lakes he found a new *Chaenactis,* a delicate member of the sunflower family. After due analysis and comparison he named it *Chaenactis alpigena*.

Another discovery was *Luzula orestera* or mountain woodrush, a distinctive little wisp with a blackish compact head. Once named it was seen to occur widely in alpine meadows, but Carl singled it out first.

In August, 1938, the same year as Helen's backpack with Annetta Carter, Carl and Helen and their friends the McIntires made what Helen called "The McIntire-Sharsmith Kaweah Expedition." With backpacks and a mule they named Balaam (also known as Little Jimmy), they traveled from Giant Forest, Sequoia National Park to the Nine Lakes Basin where they established a base camp and made day hikes in all directions. Then down the Kern Canyon to Junction Meadows, up the Kern-Kaweah River, over Colby Pass to Deadman Canyon, over Elizabeth Pass to Bearpaw Meadows, and back to Giant Forest.

In the southern Sierra Carl discovered a low hairy purple aster growing among rocks at timberline. He called it *Aster Peirsonii* for Frank Peirson, a gruff old friend and remarkable field botanist whom he had known in Pasadena during Trailfinder days.

Also down south he came upon an incredibly fragrant phlox which had never been described, and named it *Phlox dispersa*. It has pungent leaves and white clusters blooming in careless profusion amid the rotting granite of dry sand flats. Unlike any other phlox, it has underground runners between the flower cushions — a true alpine, beautiful and delicate as spiderwebs yet tough as nails.

Many another young taxonomist would have rushed into print with these additions to knowledge, but Carl hesitated. He was a perfectionist. Until he was absolutely certain that no one anywhere had found the plant before, he preferred not to publish. Time and again he went back to his flowers but

always concluded that more study
was needed and they were not quite
ready for their coming out. Years
later, when Philip A. Munz was
preparing his *A California Flora*, he
wrote urging Carl to publish his
findings so they could be included.
By then Carl's life had rushed on and
his reluctance to write had grown.
He bundled up his notes and sent
them to Munz, who duly published
them and gave Carl credit.

All that was in the future, though.
Back in Pullman, Helen was expecting a baby. She and Carl decided
they could put off completion of
their degree programs no longer.
They had never felt much at home in
the college, nor in the interesting but
alien world of the Palouse with its
prairie grasses and Columbia Basin
flora. He resigned from his position,
and in the fall of 1939 they returned
to Berkeley.

John (for John Muir) Dana was
born November 24th. By May,
1940, both Carl and Helen had their
doctorates.

Helen carrying John in the hickey, 1940.

Helen's *Flora of the Mount Hamilton Range of California* was later published. Carl's thesis, *A Contribution to the History of Alpine Flora of the Sierra
Nevada*, has never been published. Yet for scholars working in the area, it has
remained to this day a classic in its field.

18
Ranger Days in Tuolumne Meadows

> *"He was the heart of all the scene;*
> *On him the sun looked more serene;*
> *To hill and cloud his face was known —*
> *It seemed the likeness of his own;*
> *They knew by secret sympathy*
> *The public child of earth and sky."*
> — Ralph Waldo Emerson

Summer by summer, Tuolumne Meadows grew into Carl and he into them until they became an inseparable part of his being. It didn't happen immediately, nor was it happening at every moment. Only in retrospect could one see the irrevocable nature of his commitment, the impetuous and purposeful quality of it, and the deep channel his river of life was fashioning.

Carl was full of the spirit of John Muir. He had all the seriousness of a new convert frowning on levity and heretical views. Although he gave everything to his calling, at the time the results seemed intangible. Looking closely at his life then, we see daily chores, daily decisions, and daily responsibilities that hardly suggest the sweep of a grand vision. Rather, we see an earnest young ranger trying to do his duty and earn his pay. He could not have said on any given Thursday that he had changed the world. Yet like the sweet scent of flowers, his influence brought a sweetness to the mountain experience for many people.

As this continued year after year, he came to have a faithful following. He watched children grow up and their parents grow old. In time, grandchildren and even great-grandchildren of his original companions on the trail came to share the mountains with him. Many a devoted nature lover was first aroused to the beauty of the outdoors by walking with Carl.

He loved wearing the ranger's uniform. When he began serving, it consisted of white shirt, necktie, jacket, riding breeches, puttees, and British-made

field boots, all topped off by a stiff-
brimmed ranger hat. The insignia
was a wreath of leaves showing rank.
A temporary naturalist wore an animal head within the wreath, a per-
manent ranger a Sequoia cone, and
the chief ranger sported three cones.
Stars were added for each five years
of service.

As a ranger, Carl met an endless
array of exotic characters and got
along with them in one fashion or
another. Cosie Hutchings, daughter
of one of the first settlers in Yosemite
Valley, still carried on the feud
between her father and John Muir.
Hutchings had wanted to keep his
land, while Muir worked for the creation of a greatly enlarged park held
publicly for all the people. When
Carl knew her, Cosie was a little old
woman with lovely blue eyes, and so
frail it seemed a wind might blow her

*Carl demonstrating rapelling, 1950.
Photo by Art Nelson.*

away. She used to take a knapsack and go off into the back country for two or
three days at a time, scaring the living daylights out of the rangers for fear
something would happen to her. Nothing ever did.

There was the garbage woman, Hattie Bruce, a tough old girl who
chewed tobacco and spoke her mind. She was related to Jay Bruce, the State
of California mountain-lion hunter. One evening at the campfire, Ranger Bert
Harwell began eulogizing John Muir. The more he talked, the more Hattie
muttered and spat in the back row. Finally she burst out, "Oh, yeah, John
Muir, he was that guy that run off with Hutchings' wife!" The campfire
group broke up with laughter.

Another character was Doc Fahle, an expansive and generous woman who
claimed to be an Egyptologist. She gave volunteer nature walks, dispensing
mountains of misinformation about ancient glaciers flowing all the way into
San Francisco Bay, and icebergs floating out to the Hawaiian Islands. The
people loved her stories.

They loved even more the bona fide nature walks with Carl. A third of the campground usually turned out. Many of the people were used to working outdoors. They were in good physical condition and thought nothing of covering vast distances at high altitudes.

For some years Carl was the only ranger naturalist at Tuolumne Meadows, and responsible for the entire program. Yet whenever there was a crisis — a fire, a rescue — he had to pitch in and help.

During his first summer in 1931 he started leading one-week trips around the circuit of High Sierra Camps. Over time, several different routes were tried. At first the group started at Happy Isles in Yosemite, circled the high country, and returned via Mirror Lake. During a layover day at Merced Lake Carl led ambitious side trips, sometimes up the gigantic steps on the north side of Mount Clark. He found that the leader could, by his own enthusiasm, inspire others to exert themselves, and he was long on enthusiasm. Later the loop became far less strenuous, beginning and ending at Tuolumne Meadows Lodge.

For years he led a two-day trip to Waterwheel Falls, with an overnight stay at the Glen Aulin High Sierra Camp. The charge was a dollar for lodging and a dollar for dinner.

There were problems of course, such as shoes. Mountain footgear was poor in those days, and Carl learned that if he wanted people to hike with him he might have to repair their shoes. He got himself a last, awl, leather, and hobnails, and soon became a skilled cobbler.

Occasionally the problem was human. In 1933, a thirteen year old boy named Albert showed up for every walk. He was a gangling oversized kid who talked incessantly and plagued walkers and ranger alike. When it came time to climb Mount Lyell, Carl told the boy's father that Albert couldn't go. The group returned from the trip to find that Albert was missing, and a search was mounted. It continued for two days, while Carl climbed high on Lyell in a fruitless effort. Coming back exhausted and distraught late at night, he learned that the boy had hitchhiked to Placerville. But the story didn't end there. Albert's parents retrieved him, and again he began showing up for every hike, exasperating all who came along. He was so obnoxious that Carl finally prohibited him from joining the hikes for a whole week, to the temporary relief of hikers and ranger alike.

The tradition of the campfire developed gradually. At first people gathered informally at Tuolumne Lodge, while the packers strummed their guitars and everybody sang. Carl started showing up to give a little talk, but he felt like something of an intruder. Finally he and the superintendent selected a site back of the lodge tents for a naturalist's campfire. In the public campground was another campfire circle, moved several times. Eventually it was placed where it is now, in a little hollow surrounded by a close wall of trees which kept the people warm on chilly High Sierra nights. Later the opening was enlarged and the trees cut down, and it was named Dana Circle.

All the while, Helen experienced the Sierra in her own way. She loved the mountains deeply and devoted herself to learning everything she could about them. And she continued writing articles for Yosemite Nature Notes, a touch of poetry creeping in. In "Domes of Yosemite," for example, she spoke of the granite domes, the green domelike tops of Sequoia trees, and the cloud domes in the sky.

A contingent of the Civilian Conservation Corps composed of second-generation Poles from the steel and coal areas around Lake Erie was stationed in Tuolumne Meadows during the depression. These tough city kids, unused to Sierra granite, clambered up the rocks in their hobnailed army shoes yelling at each other. Carl was in mortal dread they'd slip and fall, but they never did. Occasionally he led them on an organized trip up Dana or other mountains, with a Polish-speaking sergeant along to call roll and make sure nobody strayed.

Some geologists came to Tuolumne Meadows and photographed the top of Lembert Dome. Shortly afterward Herb Ewing, District Ranger, asked Carl, "Who rolled the rocks off Lembert Dome?"

"I didn't know they were missing."

"Well, they're in those pictures the geologists took, and they aren't up there now."

They concluded the CCC boys must have done it — their idea of a lark. The boys didn't realize the boulders were irreplaceable signs of an ancient glacier.

Carl stumbled upon the pathetic victim of another "lark," a bear cub strangled by Tuolumne Lodge employees. He found the culprits vainly attempting to revive the bear with water, and although he tried artificial respiration for some time, it was to no avail.

In 1938 the Tioga Road was relocated and paved from near Tenaya Lake through Tuolumne Meadows to Tioga Pass, and the new campground opened. The number of visitors increased, and campers could no longer spread out wherever they pleased, but were herded together in the campground and more strictly controlled. The ranger naturalist's role gradually

Papa as chef, 1937.

Marie Sommer Schaarschmidt, circa 1930.

changed. He had more tenderfeet to lead now — yet no less enthusiasm, for tenderfeet love mountains too.

One of the greatest climbers of the Sierra was Norman Clyde, whom Carl had met back in 1927 on the first Trailfinder High Sierra trip. As the years passed, they occasionally crossed paths. Once Carl visited him in Los Angeles, where Clyde was living in a rented room piled high with manuscripts. The mountain man spent the afternoon griping about an editor who didn't understand his needs or his message.

In his early days, in spite of tremendous exploits, Clyde was rather scorned by other successful climbers. He had a classical college education and could read several languages, but they considered him uncouth. Later the younger climbers began to idolize him. No doubt this early disdain burned in Clyde's consciousness. Though independent and self-reliant beyond other men, he was also deeply sensitive.

In 1931 Clyde arrived in Tuolumne Meadows in his old battered Chevrolet crammed with climbing gear, to help with mountain rescues. His strength and ability were awesome. He was so big and stocky that as he strode along, Carl had to jog to keep up with him.

Together they did a first ascent of the highest Echo Peak. Clyde moved easily and quickly across the rock, never gasping with open mouth at that altitude as most people do. When they reached the top, he used a soft-nosed bullet to write a record of the climb. On the way down he taught Carl how to rappel (descend a steep face on a rope). They had been hours without a drink, and Carl's mouth was so dry he thought he would die if they didn't reach water soon. When at last they came to a creek and he gulped down great draughts, Clyde merely rinsed his mouth and spat it out.

Clyde was strong in more ways than one. After spending some time with him, Carl suggested, "Why don't you go over and have a shower?" Clyde complied, but reluctantly. Regular bathing was not part of his routine.

That summer of 1931 when Clyde was leading a group up the headwall of the glacier on Mount Conness, he stopped before a great jumble of rocks. "We got to do a little house cleaning," he announced, and set them to work clearing out the rocks to make a safer passage.

Carl always had a deep friendship for Norman and felt that he was poorly understood. He admired Clyde's knowledge of foreign languages and empathized with his passion for the mountains. When Clyde was old and unwell, he deplored unfeeling remarks made about him and mourned that his house was vandalized and his precious papers and writings scattered on the ground.

Carl had learned some climbing techniques from Clyde and had observed the development of roped climbing by the Sierra Club in the Cathedral Range. Yet as these early beginnings became a veritable craze to rope the peaks, Carl never became a part of it. He enjoyed climbing in his own way, an esthetic rather than an athletic experience, savoring the plants and animals and the vastness and beauty around him. He was fond of saying, "If there isn't a hand or foothold, don't take unfair advantage of a mountain." Anyone who has walked with him knows that he never seems to strain. No matter how far or how high he goes, he walks reverently with his eyes open.

Though he had no use for fancy climbing techniques, Carl developed considerable skill. He had his own special route up Cathedral Peak and often belayed his companions one by one from the top, urging them to climb on their own and to use the rope for security only.

It was in 1931, too, that he began taking groups on three-day trips up Mount Lyell. The first two years they had a common commissary, and Helen purchased the food. For the three days, the total cost per person for meals and mules was $1.50. By the third year, each hiker provided his own grub.

On the first day of the Lyell climb a Curry Company pack train carried everyone's equipment to Upper Base Camp. Carl and the hikers walked up in a leisurely fashion, reaching camp in time for dinner, campfire, and a good sleep. The second day they climbed the peak, Carl in the lead with ice axe, rope, and crampons. He had studied exactly where to cross the bergschrund and follow a ledge to the summit ridge. The third day was an easy hike back to Tuolumne Meadows, the mules again toting the loads.

Occasionally famous people accompanied him. One was the great geneticist Theodosius Dobzhansky with his daughter Sophie. She climbed the mountain, but her father stayed at Upper Base Camp with some rotten bananas, quite content to find out what fruit flies he might collect for his research.

The Lyell climbs were enormously popular. During the winter, Carl received reservations and made up the lists. The roster was always full. He did this every year — in later years, twice a summer — through 1957. On thirty-six ascents he never had an accident.

Carl himself was not so lucky as his companions. In 1935 he joined the Field School for their annual climb of Mount Lyell. At the summit, the party split. One group started down toward Base Camp, while Carl and a few others crossed over and ascended nearby Mount Maclure.

It was a beautiful day on the summit of Maclure. Carl had his back to the cliff as he bent to pick up a rock and examine the lichen on it. As he tugged to get it loose, suddenly something gave way. He was thrown backward over the cliff edge and began to somersault head over heels down a chute on the south slope, seeing alternate flashes of sky and ground as he rolled. His horrified companions wanted to go bounding after him, but Jules Fritsch, a Swiss ski instructor, held them back. "The whole slope's nothing but loose rock," he cautioned, "and we could do him more damage or knock him off the cliff."

The rescuers circled cautiously and came down to find Carl semi-conscious, wedged between two rocks as though seated in an armchair with his feet dangling over a 1500 foot cliff. He was bleeding from an ugly gash in the head. Someone found some black button and carpet thread in Carl's pack, and Bud Ashcraft, a medical intern, sewed up the wound in his scalp.

They devised a litter of two crooked sticks and a blanket, and organized a relay with people stationed along the mountain to take turns carrying him. Word was sent ahead, and those who had already reached camp prepared soup and sent it up for the rescue crew, while others carried up wood to light fires along the route.

In his state of shock, Carl was chilled to the bone. It had grown dark by

the time they carried him across the glacier deeply pitted by sun cups. Each
time one of the bearers slipped and went down, Carl was slammed against the
frozen snow. The cold cut him like a knife.

He intermittently regained consciousness and noticed at one point that his
rescuers were taking the wrong route. He waved his head and tried to tell
them, "There's a gap in the moraine, go through there, it's easier that way."

"Oh, yeah, oh, yeah," they answered, but paid no attention. They thought
he was out of his head. Assuming they had taken his advice, Carl wondered
why they were having such a difficult time getting down.

After many hours they arrived in camp, and Carl, only semi-conscious and
in pain, was put to sleep on an air mattress offered by one of the women. He
had scorned this recent invention as sissy, but it felt like fluffy clouds after his
harrowing ride.

In the morning a CCC crew came up and carried him to the roadhead,
where an ambulance was waiting to take him to the Yosemite Hospital. He
spent a month there. Helen, who was studying for her PhD qualifying exams,
divided the time between study in her tent in Yosemite Valley and visits with
Carl. Then he was transferred to the United States Marine Hospital in San
Francisco for another month. The doctors were never certain whether he had
broken any bones, but his entire body had received a wrenching from which
it took long to recover.

Helen passed her exams. When Carl finally returned home that autumn of
1935, she had two gifts for him: a new green Ford V-8 roadster which he
promptly named The Jimmy Car, and tickets to the dress circle at the opera
to hear the Wagnerian Ring. For these occasions, Helen sewed herself a beautiful green dress and green velvet opera cape to set off her red hair. They
made each opera a celebration of Carl's recovery and of their joy at being
together.

The following summer Carl was back in the meadows without even a scar
to show for his ordeal, enjoying the mountains as never before after having
almost lost them forever.

19
Ranger Days Continued:
Wider Yosemite

Although he was to be identified with Tuolumne Meadows most of his life, Carl came to know and love all of Yosemite and to serve it in many capacities over the years. Each year the Park Service tried to delay the opening of the Tioga Road to Tuolumne Meadows so that the surface would dry out and cars wouldn't tear it up too badly. Until the road opening, Carl was given other assignments. Thus he worked in all the entrance stations, the Mariposa Big Trees Grove, Glacier Point, and on many occasions Yosemite Valley.

From the Valley he led all day hikes to Sierra Point, Grizzly Point, Yosemite Falls, Half Dome, and elsewhere, almost always with a crowd. When he arrived in the morning at the old Yosemite Lodge, he might find as many as a hundred people sitting on the front porch and perched on the polished railings waiting to go to the top of the falls. On the way up he would stop at the zigzags for trail talks so as to be heard by his long line of followers above and below.

Sometimes he was assigned the daily auto caravan which circled the upper end of the valley in the morning and the lower end in the afternoon. In June the mosquitoes could be fierce in spite of mosquito control, and stops were often cut short by attacks of insect squadrons.

On other mornings he gave the nine o'clock ranger talk, worked at the desk, and lectured again at eleven. Occasionally he worked in the forestry room making labels or preparing skins for the park mammal collection. Afternoons he helped at the Indian show in back of the museum. A popular performer was Lemee, a Miwok Indian, who danced with jingling bells on his ankles and feathers on his head. In his desire to look impressive he occasionally wore a Sioux war bonnet; the rangers argued with him and finally persuaded him to dress as an authentic Miwok. With his ear for music, Carl soon learned Lemee's chants.

As part of the show, Tabuce, an older Yosemite Indian woman, ground acorns on a stone, rinsed them in a basket to leach out the tannins, and baked acorn patties on a flat rock. She also cooked mush in a basket by dropping hot stones into ground acorns and water. Once when she ran out of stones she asked Carl to find her some more.

"There's nothing to that," he thought. Knowing that many rocks would break apart when heated, he carefully selected hard, fine-grained specimens with no apparent cracks, and proudly presented them to her. Tabuce sat on the ground in front of the pile and picked one up.

"Him no good." She tossed it aside and chose another. "Him no good." A third. "Him okay." How she knew was a mystery Carl never fathomed.

After working all day, Carl frequently gave a program at the big campfire circle. It had a large stage and seats for about five hundred people. He always experienced a little stage fright, but learned that it would pass. At that time a popular radio show was "Amateur Hour," and the rangers began staging an imitation during the evening campfire. They were supposed to audition applicants and select the best, but their efforts must have been sketchy. Some of the acts were terrible. Carl was never involved in the screening but now and then served as Master of Ceremonies. He didn't like it much. He had joined the Park Service because of his love of nature, not to run ham shows. Nevertheless he tried to do his best.

The Firefall followed the naturalist's talk. A large fire of red fir bark would have been burning on Glacier Point all evening. When the entertainment at Camp Curry ended, the call went up into the night, "Is the fire ready?"

Everyone waited in hushed anticipation until a voice from Glacier Point replied, "The fire is ready." Then from below, "LET THE FIRE FALL!" At this, the burning embers were pushed over the cliff creating a showy cascade of glowing coals.

The ranger naturalists at their campfire could never tell when the Firefall would take place, and even if the naturalist was smack in the middle of his presentation, everyone would get up and leave.

Each night after the Firefall the tourists jumped into their cars and drove to the lower end of the Valley to see the bears, creating so much traffic that rangers with flashlights had to direct at the intersections. The spectators' area was on the south side of the Merced River, and by the time it filled, the sky had become quite dark. A lane was left from the road to the stump where the naturalist gave his talk. The last to arrive was the big bus from the Ahwahnee, which chugged right up to the back of the stump.

When all was ready, the naturalist reached down and turned on big floodlights illuminating the other side of the river. There, where the hotel garbage had been dumped, were the bears — sometimes as many as twenty. At that moment all the people up and down the river released a collective "Ahhhh!" like wind blowing through the pine trees. And then the naturalist gave his talk.

The first time it was Carl's turn, he went to the library and read up on the habits of bears. He knew very little about them, but with a smatter-ing from books he was able to mud-dle through a ten minute talk.

The summer cabin in Tuolumne Meadows, 1946.

The next morning he was working at the desk in the museum when Colonel Thomson, the rough, tough superintendent of the park, came by. Carl admired him enormously. The superintendent had formerly been sta-tioned in Missouri in the branch of the army that supplied mules to the caval-ry. Like an old cavalryman he chewed cigars in the corner of his mouth, and gave the spittoons a running business. No one could tell when or where Thomson might turn up, for he took an interest in everything in the park.

Mouthing the usual cigar, the colonel came over to the desk, and Carl stood at attention. "Well, Sharsmith," he drawled, "I was down at the bear pits last night."

"Yes, Colonel Thomson."

He spat. "Yeah, I heard your talk." A long pause, and another expectora-tion. "And...it...was...lousy!"

During the Second World War Carl accompanied a detatchment of about a hundred soldiers for a drive to Glacier Point, where he gave a talk about geol-ogy. The talk was going well when someone came in at the back and yelled, "Hey, you guys, they're serving free beer by the hotel." All interest in geology eroded in a general stampede.

That morning Ansel Adams had told Carl, "When you're on your way back, I'll station myself at the east end of the Wawona Tunnel. I'd like to have a picture of you and the officers coming out of the tunnel in the lead car."

Carl kept this in mind. He was riding with the commanding officer in the lead car on the return trip, when suddenly an automobile went by at terrific speed. Carl dutifully pulled the driver over for a reprimand, while the rest of the caravan passed them by. When, last in line, they finally emerged from the tunnel, he saw Ansel waiting patiently and waving his big black veil to get them to stop for the picture.

While Carl was stationed at Glacier Point, Eleanor Roosevelt came to visit. As she fed the ground squirrels, he lacked the courage to tell her it was against the rules. Then the other visitors were kept back, and he and Mrs. Roosevelt walked to the edge of the cliff. "I want to see where the Firefall goes down," she said.

He answered, "We can look very briefly, but at this time of morning there's an updraft and we may get our eyes full of cinders." She insisted, and he turned out to be right. Even with cinders in her eyes, the genial first lady was impressed by the view.

Mountain rescues — an important part of a ranger's duties — were exciting and sometimes scary. Whenever word came that someone was in trouble, the rangers dashed off in their shirt sleeves without wasting a minute. One evening as it was getting dark an eighteen year old girl was reported caught in Tenaya Canyon.

She and her younger sister had left Tuolumne Meadows and had tried to take a short cut down the canyon to Yosemite Valley. They got as far as the brink of a waterfall, and managed to worm their way down beside it. Not far from the bottom of the fall, the older girl slipped and injured her foot. They were trapped in an inaccessible box canyon, and the younger sister had to work her way back up a narrow ledge along one side of Mount Watkins to get help.

Carl was assigned a group of Curry Company employees and told to go up and get her. It was pitch dark when the party finally reached the gorge. They climbed a wall to the lower end of the little box valley, along ledges slanting outward. Soon they came to Tenaya Creek, filling the gorge to its impassable sides. Carl realized this was probably where, years before, Muir had slipped and fallen on his way to Tenaya Lake. They found the girl and made her as comfortable as they could, built a big fire, and stayed all night. In the morning rangers from the Valley arrived with ropes and a Stokes litter. They rigged up guy lines tight above and beneath, and made a device like an aerial tramway to hold the litter. The injured girl was tied in with her head pointed downhill to keep the weight of her body off the foot, and slowly lowered to the canyon floor.

The next day Carl went back to look at the site and was appalled. In the dark he hadn't been able to see the three hundred foot drop below the slanting ledges they had climbed.

One day in May, Carl had a group with him on Half Dome. It was cloudy, and the cap of the dome was wet with sludgy snow. As they were about to go down the ladder, the woman ahead of him called, "Oh, ranger, look at the lizard!"

He picked it up — a beautiful little thing, all shiny black with dots of pure gold. It seemed like a lizard, but what would a lizard be doing out in the snow in weather like this?

Suddenly he had a wild idea. Could it be a Mount Lyell salamander? He had seen it in a book, but never alive. Discovered on Mount Lyell in 1915, the two caught at that time were the only known specimens.

He carefully collected some wet moss to keep the creature from drying out and sent it to Dr. Charles L. Camp, the Berkeley paleontologist who had originally described the Mount Lyell salamander. In due time a note came back. Carl's hunch had been correct, and the Mount Lyell salamander had now been rediscovered.

Since then these amphibians have turned up at the base and upper end of Yosemite Falls, and many have been seen on Half Dome. Their entire skin must be kept moist, so they lurk in wet places and are rarely noticed. Once Carl found one by groping around under the Icy Monkey Flower by a cold stream in an alpine meadow. They remain rare and elusive and a great mystery historically, as their closest known relatives are on the Mediterranean island of Sardinia — an unlikely place for a Sierran animal to find its cousins.

20
Minnesota

I t was 1940, and at last Carl and Helen were the Doctors Sharsmith, now fully prepared for university teaching. But although Helen had labored long and hard for her degree, there was no thought of her going to work. Their son John had been born the previous November.

Carl hoped fervently that he could find a position in California in order to be close to his beloved High Sierra. He was disappointed when his faculty advisor, Dr. Mason, found him a job in the botany department of the University of Minnesota. Still, teaching positions were hard to come by, the University was an excellent institution, and there seemed no alternative. He felt he was signing his heart away.

Now Carl was torn from the place where he wanted to be and cast into a new alienation with a strange new biota, and no mountains for hundreds of miles in any direction. The highest point in Minneapolis was the top of the tall office building where his dentist presided. Had he never known the Sierra he might have taken to the nearby north woods, the legendary land from which many of his friends in the lumber camps hailed, but he could not make the transition.

Each year the Sharsmiths arrived in the fall after a summer in the Sierra, and no sooner had school started and the asters come into bloom than winter closed down. Then, after what seemed an interminable time of ice and snow, it all melted off and hot summertime arrived.

Helen had her hands full taking care of her first-born. It was some time before they discovered John had an ear infection. Placed in the hospital, he got his arm caught in the crib and broke a collar bone.

Helen continued to help Carl in his work, and somehow kept up with her own studies. He admired her capability and seemed unaware that there might be ways in which her life could be more satisfying. Remembering his mother and her immersion in her domestic and maternal role, he assumed that Helen would be the same — with the addition that she could understand and help in his professional life.

They took occasional trips into the surrounding Minnesota countryside. Carl collected plants whenever he had an opportunity, and made some new plant acquaintances like the spotted-touch-me-not or jewel weed, which seemed curious and laughable to him. When he touched it, bing! the seed pod exploded.

Once or twice they went camping. Berry Campbell, professor of anatomy, went with them and brought along his wife and four children. Whenever the children found any bones, their father made a game of putting them together. They even collected and articulated the entire skeleton of a horse.

The Sharsmiths went ice skating and hiked in the snow, towing John in an apple box tied onto a sled. They tried skiing, but Carl's old knee injury from the lumber camps kept him from becoming a proficient skier.

Carl respected many of his colleagues, but he did not develop lasting friendships. His heart was elsewhere. Yet he profitted by getting to know Dr. William Skinner Cooper, the plant ecologist whose ideas had long interested him. Also Dr. Frederick King Butters, a mountaineer who had made some first ascents in the Selkirks with the American Alpine Club, and was very much a Harvard man with a marked New England accent. When Butters lectured about the sword fern, his students wrote down "sawed fern" and gave it back that way on the test. He seemed to know everything there was to know in botany and was often consulted about botanical mysteries no one else could unravel.

Another colleague was Dr. Ernst Abbe, professor of plant anatomy and morphology. His father was a noted climatologist who had devised a way to eliminate chromatic aberration in microscopes.

Carl once went ice climbing with ice axe, ice pitons and crampons along the sandstone cliffs bordering the Mississippi River with Dr. Stacy French, a plant physiologist who was later head of the Plant Biology Section of the Carnegie Institution at Stanford. French had learned his technique in the Alps. But such excursions were rare. Once in a while Carl and Helen went into the field with Dr. Rosendahl, the department chairman. Rosendahl had studied with Dr. Engler, a world-famous Berlin botanist at the *Berliner Botanischergarten*. To the regret of botanists everywhere, this famous botanical garden was shortly to be destroyed in the Second World War.

Carl gave a course in taxonomy and one on economic plants. In those days it was possible to write to various companies that dealt in fibers, resins, pharmaceuticals, tannins, etc., and they would send generous samples of their raw

materials. In the basement of the pharmacy building Carl discovered bales
and sacks of crude drugs from all over the world. Using these as a base, and
with Helen writing far and wide for additional samples, he built up an excellent museum of economic plants.

Each summer they piled into the little roadster and headed west. The summer of 1940 was spent in Tuolumne Meadows. With John less than a year
old, Helen entered a new phase. No longer free to hike as she pleased, she
found it difficult to keep up with the laundry, baking, mending, cooking,
baby-sitting and paper work. Suddenly she felt confined, unable to enjoy the
high country as she had always done. She had to carry John along in his
Paiute baby carrier (called a hickey) when she hiked. At summer's end she
added up the number of trips taken: six. Although she did not have time to
write about most of them, the last, to Shepherd's Crest, she described in a
sparkling article in Yosemite Nature Notes.

The next summer, 1941, Carl was assigned as the first ranger-naturalist at
Cedar Grove in Kings Canyon National Park. He threw himself into the
work, developing a program as he had in Tuolumne and enticing people to
follow him up every possible trail. On his days off he often explored new
routes.

His work was much appreciated, and Helen was proud of him. However,
for her it was another frustrating summer. John was now a twenty-two pound
toddler, and it seemed that she spent all her time washing, ironing with
sadirons, cooking, cleaning, and looking after him. At first she was delighted
with the canyon, but after a while she felt imprisoned, far from the high country she loved so well. "If I don't get at least a look-see soon, I'll develop claus-
trophobia down here where I can only 'Ce-dar Grove,'" she punned. Carl
was busy with his walks and climbs, and in order to go along she had to carry
John in the hickey. She managed it on a fourteen mile overnight hike to
Paradise Valley, but the baby was wakeful during the night and Carl was
annoyed. She wrote, "An improvement will have to be made in John's sleeping arrangements, or no more back country for him and me." As Carl prepared for another hike to Monarch Divide she complained, "I am despondent
that I cannot go too."

In late July when Jane McIntire and her father came to visit, they traveled
with Helen and John and a mule as far into the backcountry as Junction
Meadow and East Lake. Helen was ecstatic.

The United States entered the Second World War, but because of his age
and family status Carl was never drafted. At the University, he saw his students

Carl with Linnea and John, 1944. Photo by Helen Sharsmith.

going off to war and felt the sorrow when some of them were killed in unreal far-away places. For him the politics of war and the international chaos came as eerie echoes from a world he neither knew nor wished to be part of. His reality was in his plants, his family, and his mountains.

Even in the mountains things were not the same. At Tuolumne Meadows in 1942, fewer people came because of gas rationing. By 1943 the park administration decided it no longer needed a ranger-naturalist in Tuolumne. Carl still returned each year to Yosemite, but he filled in as a general ranger manning an entrance station or working on patrol in the valley.

On December 28, 1942, a daughter was born to the Sharsmiths. They named her Linnea after the flower honoring the great Swedish botanist. Now Helen carried Linnea on her back in the hickey as she took John to nursery school on a sled. When Linnea became a toddler, Helen pulled them both, snugly bundled up in their snowsuits against the bitter weather. They had to cross the Mississippi River on a bridge where the winds were so strong they one day blew Carl's hat off and carried it away down the river.

In the summer of 1944, Park Naturalist Frank Brockman arranged with the Yosemite Natural History Association for Carl to receive a grant of one hundred dollars to make a collection of Yosemite plants. Helen and the children lived in a tent in Camp Six, while he hiked all over the park to many of the remote unvisited spots, and filled the park herbarium with many new specimens.

His Indian friend Tabuce was getting old. She no longer worked. She lived on Paiute land on Farington's ranch at the foot of Bloody Canyon near Lee Vining. Injured in childhood by a falling tree, she limped badly when she walked. On one occasion Carl brought her up to Tuolumne Meadows for a visit and an overnight in his tent. It was during a time of sugar rationing. At dinner Carl pushed the sugar bowl across to her, and she pushed it right back. "Me got some," Tabuce said and went out to the truck for her own coffee sugar.

During the summer, Carl and his family went down several times to take Tabuce some groceries. She lived in a tiny house with a willow wickiup along-side; she preferred the wickiup and its pile of sheepskins to the alien comfort of the house. On one visit she gave the children toys she had made for them — a doll for each in a tiny hickey. For John it was a boy with zigzag lightning woven into the hood; for Linnea, the rhombic patterns proper for girls. Another time, Tabuce hobbled inside, groped around the cabin, and came out with a bag of piñon nuts for Helen. Some were as big as almonds.

"Tabuce," she exclaimed, "where did you get those?"

"Me no tell."

Again Tabuce went inside and brought out a greasy little flour sack with ka-cha-vee in the bottom. She knew Carl liked this traditional Mono Indian dish that tastes like shrimp and is made of the larvae of a brine fly that lives along the shores of Mono Lake.

As they left, Carl and Helen said, "Well, Tabuce, we'll see you again next year."

"No, you no see me no more."

"Nonsense, Tabuce. You'll be around for years and years."

"No more," Tabuce repeated. She was right. Although she seemed in good health, by the following spring she was dead.

In time the war ended. At Minnesota Helen had spent evening after evening writing letters of application for Carl to California colleges, but to no avail. Sometimes the yearning was so poignant that Carl wept. Finally in 1946 he could withstand his feelings no longer. With no job in sight, he resigned from the University of Minnesota, and for the last time he and his family made the trek home to California.

Tuolumne Meaows seemed to welcome him back with special radiance. Blue sky pilot bloomed all over the top of Mount Dana in undisturbed profusion. This was where Carl Sharsmith belonged.

Leaves

The Sharsmith Family at home in Menlo Park, 1947. Photo by Helen Sharsmith.

21
Alone

"Murmur, a little sadly, how love fled
And paced upon the mountains overhead
And hid his face amid a crowd of stars."
— William Butler Yeats

I t had now been six years since Carl had completed his thesis. He had
long wanted to revise it for publication, and upon leaving the
University of Minnesota he was determined to do so. After spending
some time collecting plants in Minnesota and Wisconsin, he and his
family drove west to Tuolumne Meadows, and then visited the grandparents
in Tujunga before returning to the Bay Area. Helen, who always managed
the money, bought a little house in Menlo Park so they could be near the
Dudley Herbarium at Stanford which housed many of the reference materials
Carl needed.

Every morning he left the little house and spent long hours in the herbarium. Dr. Roxanne Ferris, who had worked with Abrams on his monumental
Illustrated Flora of the Pacific States, was in charge. She found a desk for Carl
where he could work undisturbed. But the work went slowly as he painstakingly reviewed each section and restudied each plant. He was a perfectionist.
He couldn't allow anything to go out over his name which did not satisfy him
in every detail. As the seasons turned from summer to winter to summer
again, he forgot everything else, and several years went by.

Each year the family summered in Tuolumne Meadows. Carl's ranger's
salary was their only income through the year.

In 1948 a terrible forest fire broke out on Rancheria Mountain above Pate
Valley. All the rangers were called to fight it, Carl among them. They stayed
on the site for three weeks, exhausted by arduous work, short of rations, and
always short of sleep.

A number of Yosemite Indians were working the fire line with them. One
of the boys, Ralph Parker, had eyes like a hawk. He would point, "There's the

fire. Can't you see it?" No one else could, but when the smoke swelled and
the flames spread, they knew he was right. Ralph's father, Lloyd, was known
as Dad Parker. In the middle of the night as the fire fighters slept exhausted
right where they were working, they sometimes woke to hear the scraping of
a shovel: Dad Parker putting out a blaze.

Dad helped the Park Service in other ways. Once a Field School group was
returning from climbing Mount Lyell along the Lyell Fork of the Tuolumme
River when a ten-year-old boy ran up shouting, "Help! My buddy's fallen
into the river!"

Carl and the others searched up and down the stream but found nothing.
As he and Dad Parker were standing on a granite boulder, Dad said, "Here,
hold me by the belt and I'll look under this rock." Carl clutched tight as Dad
edged down and found the boy's lifeless body. With this tragedy fresh in his
mind, Carl had to hurry back to the lodge to give a campfire and sing happy
songs with the campers.

Each fall Carl returned to Menlo Park to spend long hard hours on his
thesis revision. In 1949 he also agreed to revise and update Ansel Hall's
Yosemite Flora. But nine months later it remained untouched, as he lost himself in his work at the herbarium.

Striving to make both ends meet, Helen took a job with the Carnegie
Institution at Stanford University as assistant to a research team. It was not
full time, and she began to worry about money. Their resources were shrink-
ing before her eyes, and Carl had no job and apparently no intention of getting one. Gradually Helen became deeply depressed, as she found she could
no longer talk freely with a husband who was totally immersed in his work
and seemed unaware of other realities.

In the summer of 1950 when Carl returned to Tuolumne Meadows,
Helen chose to go her separate way. She was almost immediately appointed
senior herbarium botanist at the University of California Herbarium in
Berkeley and remained there until her retirement in 1969.

She moved to a house on Chestnut Street in Berkeley, and Carl came to
visit her and the children from time to time. He sometimes took John to the
mountains with him, and tried to make the children feel that they had a
father. He gave much thought to the toys he now and then brought them,
and recorded in his journal, "John, yellow dump truck, garbage truck, ambulance, motor car; Linnea, a little girl doll with hair wig, not a baby doll."

Helen entered upon an active life of work and research and home. She had
become interested in *Hesperolinon,* a rather obscure genus in the flax family

that grows only on serpentine rock and is found widely in California. On many a weekend she went camping in various parts of the state, frequently with John as companion, collecting *Hesperolinons,* building campfires in secluded hollows, and taking plunges in ponds and rivers on long hot afternoons. In the summers she alternated special trips with John and Linnea, often with the Sierra Club, always arranging for the other child to go to summer camp or to be with friends. In this way each of her children had ongoing opportunities to enjoy the outdoors. They rarely went back to Tuolumne Meadows, however, and long afterwards Helen wrote, "In 1950 I left half my heart there."

After nineteen years of marriage, the separation from Helen was a deep sorrow to Carl. He honored her for her fine mind and for all the help she had given him, and he hoped they might some day be reunited. In the meantime, his thesis revision limped along more and more slowly. His heart had gone out of it.

Carl now faced the future alone. A whole chapter of his life was closed, and a new one was opening up. He went at it, if not with the joy of his younger self, at least with a determination to do his best. At the moment it was all he could muster.

At first he stayed with various friends, and then Jeff McBride (a well-known taxonomist working on the flora of Peru for the Chicago Field Museum) invited Carl to share a house in the Santa Cruz Mountains. He continued trying to complete the rewrite, sometimes sleeping on the Stanford grounds under the trees in order to have longer days in the herbarium.

One day as Carl was grinding away, Dr. Carl Duncan, Chairman of the Department of Biological Sciences at San Jose State College, dropped in. He knew of Carl's work and asked, "Do you need a job?"

"Yes, as a matter of fact I do." It was decided on the spot that Carl would teach at San Jose State.

Academically, it was something of a comedown for Carl. Minnesota was a prestigious university, and San Jose State primarily a teachers' college. Accustomed to working with upper division and graduate students, he was taken aback to be assigned to teach nature study to prospective teachers. "I don't see myself telling bedtime stories about plants," he grumbled.

He also taught botany, plant geography, and geographical plant ecology. But year in and year out, his main course, required for biology majors, was taxonomy. Something of an academic missionary, he gave it everything he had of rigor and precision. He always regretted that taxonomy was not a year-long course, insisting he couldn't cover the subject properly in less. During the single semester allotted, he required that students learn to handle a botanical key and know how to collect and prepare specimens. There was a body of knowledge and competence to be mastered, and he was determined that they do so. Those who fell short felt his disapproval keenly. Those who succeeded looked back with gratitude and affection on a course they could have found in few other places. Carl stood for no nonsense and wasted little time on "appreciation." His role models were the many exacting professors who had earned his respect even as he quaked in his boots before them.

Appreciation was exactly the kind of thing he taught so well in Tuolumne Meadows. But he approached his academic work differently from his role as ranger-naturalist. In the Meadows he wore his ranger uniform, and when off duty, clean patched hiking clothes. He taught college in professorial jacket, shirt, and tie. With these changes of envelope came subtle changes in personality. Throughout his life he had striven to live fully the responsibilities and role of the moment, from rough-and-ready woodsman to painstaking student, to rigorous professor, to genial ranger-naturalist. They added up to not one but several personae. Each role contained something of Carl, yet each was a mask concealing something of Carl. Thus he was known to many, but few or none knew him in his true complexity.

There was an interesting parallel between his role as professor and his role as ranger-naturalist in Tuolumne Meadows. In the meadows, too, he was a missionary — but his gospel was love and appreciation. In each role he came to exemplify to an extraordinary degree what he taught.

Had life presented the opportunity, Carl might have taught literature or music with equal authenticity. Did his students suspect that as he ate his solitary dinner he was reading English or German poetry? That he could quote pages of Shakespeare and Goethe verbatim, and talk for hours of their rhythm, their language, their metaphors? Did they guess that he could sing many operatic arias which he had learned from records? Each of these other unlived lives would also have been a mask, a persona, a partial truth.

One day in San Jose Carl noticed a tiny house for sale for three thousand dollars. Since he was living in a furnished room, he bought the little place. Not long thereafter, as he walked back and forth to the college, he discovered a cottage only a block away on St. James Street which appealed to him even more. He sold the first house and bought the cottage. It was just right, with a livingroom, a little breakfast nook soon transformed into an office, a kitchen, bathroom, bedroom, and garage. He had space to store his books, spread out his specimens, and cook his frugal meals. There was a carpet on the floor, but after some years he took it up and discovered a beautiful parqueted hardwood floor which he refinished.

In the front room he assembled a watercolor of Mount Dana by Don Louis Percival, a photo of the Matterhorn by Harry James, a photograph of Muir by Charles Fletcher Lummis, an oil painting of a southwestern mountain, and finally a group of shots of himself and his followers and companions on the trail. In the bedroom hung pictures of John, Linnea, and Helen. The several plaques and other honors he had received were packed away in boxes.

At first he found his new neighborhood rather rowdy, but as more and more Portuguese moved in, it grew to be a clean and tidy little community. Most of his neighbors were from the Azores. On their *festa* days Carl loved to watch the children in native costume march along the street to the nearby Church of the Seven Wounds.

He built upon the record collection he had started with Helen, and gradually amassed compositions from Vivaldi and Mozart through Beethoven and Brahms. Many of his records are operas; the fine old voices give him much pleasure in the evenings after work.

In establishing his new way of life, he bought a second-hand Raleigh bicycle in 1956 and took to riding it the three miles to school. When school ended, the little Jimmy Car Helen had bought him so long ago carried him to Tuolumne Meadows. In the fall it brought him back, to snooze away in hibernation in the garage for another winter while Carl rode the bike.

He felt keenly the loss of his children. In the midst of a busy life he had always valued their company. Now the relationship was attenuated, his visits with them brief and infrequent. When he did see the children he tried to make it a happy occasion, a celebration. Yet often the visits were tinged with a deep sadness.

For high school, Carl and Helen cooperated to send John and Linnea to Verde Valley, a private school in Sedona, Arizona. Like his father before him, Carl hoped that one or both would choose to follow in his and Helen's footsteps. But, just as he had done, they would walk their own ways and follow their own trails.

22
Mountain Solace

*"For nature ever faithful is
To such as trust her faithfulness."*
— Ralph Waldo Emerson

It was fortunate for Carl at the time of separation from Helen that he had his work at Tuolumne. The mountains had always been a joy to him, and now they were a solace. Sunshine gleaming on glacial polish, the elegant unfolding of a fern leaf, the intense purposeful busyness of meadow voles and nesting mountain bluebirds swept him back into the great natural rhythms of the earth, and he was grateful.

He found, too, human warmth. Each season he greeted old friends who had been walking with him for years, and each season he made new friends. The responsibility of having these eager faces and inquiring minds depending upon him took him out of himself.

When John was about eleven, he accompanied Carl and his old friend Stacy French, now at the Carnegie Institution at Stanford, up the Dana Glacier. Stacy belayed Carl as he climbed about sixty feet down a crevasse, while John waited in the snow playing climber, with a string around his ankle tied symbolically to an ice axe.

All this time Carl had been in charge of the entire naturalist program in Tuolumne Meadows. Now and then he would ask the chief naturalist, "Am I doing all right?"

The answer always came back, "Yes, Carl, go right ahead. You're doing fine."

After the Second World War, many more people came to Tuolumne Meadows, and the naturalist program was expanded to meet the need. About 1950 a second ranger-naturalist, Allan Waldo, was added to the staff, soon to be supplemented by two more, Will Neely and Alan Shields. There was often a fifth naturalist who changed from year to year — and plenty of work for all of them.

Waldo was a genial geologist with a PhD from Harvard; in the winter he taught at Stockton College and the University of the Pacific. He and his wife Cherrie had a tent in back of the contact station and returned summer after summer for many years with their two daughters.

Alan Shields was professor of philosophy at San Diego State College in the wintertime. In summer he gave himself to the meadows and mountains with the same passion he gave to ideas.

Will Neely had an unusual gift for teaching. He got people to stand on their heads to see the light shining through the meadow flowers, or to

Will Neely, 1950. Photo by Ralph Anderson, courtesy of the NPS.

take off their shoes and stockings and feel the mud on their feet when crossing a river. Once coming down from Vogelsang Lake he told his group to lie down and look across the frozen expanse of Evelyn Lake. "Now you can see the prehistoric Tuolumne Glacier stretching from here all the way to the mountains on the other side."

Some people said of Will, "He's a second Carl." This irritated Will, who didn't think he was a second anybody. From then on he insisted on doing everything differently to proclaim his independence. In spite of a certain competition between them, Carl and Will developed a warm friendship and worked happily together for many years.

The number of activities for visitors expanded greatly in the almost endless variety of the Yosemite high country, and the public responded with enthusiasm. By the 1950's the naturalists were conducting over fifty different all-day hikes each season. (See Appendix for a list.) However, their plans were anything but formal. If the meadows were boggy, they climbed the peaks; if the peaks were too stormy they strolled in the woods. They decided day by day where to go, each day a fresh and exciting discovery of the changing face of the mountain world.

Allan Waldo led a geology car caravan over Tioga Pass, down to Mono Lake, and finally up to Walker Lake at the foot of Bloody Canyon. He gave talks on the landforms and processes observed along the way. Meanwhile one of the other naturalists led an all day hike over Mono Pass and down Bloody Canyon to meet him.

Years later Carl remembered these many trips with a warm glow, and sometimes a little smile. He recalled the time a group of sixty showed up for a climb of Mount Conness — including one woman in high heels. There was another woman who came with the rangers every day and talked incessantly until her fellow hikers, and Carl too, became sick of her. One day on Tuolumne Peak she set up her usual call, "Oh, Ranger, come here and see this flower!"

"There she goes again," thought Carl. But when he obediently ambled over, he saw she had discovered something never before found in Yosemite: *Veronica cusickii* from northeastern Oregon with a blossom almost as large as a quarter. Its Yosemite relatives are much less showy.

Carl learned patience over the years, withholding critical comments and trying to accept people as they are. He knew his own moods, his stage fright at campfires which no one suspected, his inner irritation at what he considered transgressions. He felt he had to watch himself and practice self-control, and learned his lesson well, developing an easy, gracious personality. The fierce evangelizing fire became a warm philosophical glow.

Always concerned for safety, he led thousands of people on hikes and almost invariably brought his group back without accident. There were two exceptions. Once on Tuolumne Peak a man had a moment of vertigo on a slanting ledge and fell and broke his ankle. Another time on Polly Dome, a young boy disregarded Carl's instructions to stay off the treacherous snow and on the rock. Sure enough, he started to slide and ended up at the bottom with a fractured leg. On both occasions the rangers made speedy and successful rescues. Although he was in no way at fault, Carl regretted these two incidents, wondering if he might have prevented them.

Carl had a very close call himself. He went out alone in the late fifties to reconnoiter the north side of Polly Dome in order to assess the possibility of rerouting the road away from the shores of Lake Tenaya. While working along a ledge, he touched a log. It began to roll toward him. He jumped clear just in time to escape being crushed.

One of his favorite climbs was the Columbia's Finger back of the Sunrise High Sierra Camp. It has joint planes in the rock like steps, and on one of the highest steps grows the beautiful and seldom-seen blue and yellow *Polemonium pulcherrimum*. He worried that climbers might trample them,

Exploring the ice cave in Dana Glacier, 1951. Photo by H.E. Mehden.

but rejoiced over the years to find they remained undamaged.

After World War II, Carl noticed that Tuolumne Meadows was swarming with little kids. He instituted the highly succesful nature walks for younger children, and longer hikes for the eight- to ten-year-olds. Their parents fixed them knapsacks and lunches, and Carl led them on all-day rambles to such spots as Little Devil's Post Pile. On the way back they would sit down in a natural room among the trees while he told them Indian stories, old fairy tales, or animal experiences. Then he played his harmonica.

Once a doe suddenly poked her head through the thicket right above the children's heads. Carl said, "Shhh!" and kept on playing, while the children listened breathless. Then they heard, "trrp, trrp, trrp," while she trotted around to another side and stuck her head in again. Then, "trrp, trrp, trrp," to a third side while the children gazed in wonder. Strangely, the same thing happened again the following week with another group of children.

About four in the afternoon as they came near the parking lot where their parents were waiting, Carl would have the children get down on all fours and sneak up, jump to their feet, whoop like Indians, and yell, "We're going to scalp you!"

He stressed to the children how easily things in nature are lost through the carelessness of people with their big clumsy feet. He talked about the wild ani-

mals, their life histories, and how vulnerable they are to the vagaries of existence — our fellow mortals, as Muir said, just like people.

Like any bureaucracy, the Park Service was not always easy to work for.
Sometimes a new boss decided to turn everything topsy-turvy. Staff meetings
could be a bore. "We're all squared away and rounded off," Will used to say
in disgust. And park policy did not provide promotions for summer rangers.
Thus after fifty years of work Carl was classified at the same pay grade at
which he started.

Sometimes the system got its wires crossed. An order came down for Carl
to climb Mount Dana and paint orange dots to mark the route. He post-
poned it as long as he could, but one windy day he took a bucket of paint and
did the dirty job, trying to paint on loose rock wherever he could.

It was no sooner done than Chief Ranger Carl Danner heard about it and
went to Superintendent Carl Russell. "How long will those paint spots last?"
he asked.

"Oh, about a hundred years," was the answer.

"Well," said Danner, "we've got to get that guy to remove them." So Carl
was sent up again. This time he tried to turn over as many of the rocks as he
could to hide the paint. It wasn't possible to cover them all, however, and
some of the orange spots show to this day.

Whatever frustrations there were, Carl put up with them in order to keep
coming back to Tuolumne Meadows. And the Park Service was not unmind-
ful of his devotion. In 1956 he was awarded the Department of the Interior's
silver medal for "meritorious service."

He was pleased by the award, and happy that he had earned it doing exactly what he wanted to do all his life long. Nevertheless, there would come a
time when he would be separated from Tuolumne for two long seasons.

23
Saving the Meadows

*"That existence is surely contemptible which regards only
the gratification of instinctive want and the preservation
of a body made to perish."* — Carl Linnaeus

O ne day Lowell Sumner, a renowned wildlife specialist for the
national parks, and Russ Grater, a Yosemite ranger, came to see
Carl at his house in San Jose. The Park Service had a problem.
Mountain meadows throughout the Sierra were deteriorating.
In many areas overuse by pack stock produced great ruts which destroyed
meadow sod and washed out standing water, thus lowering the water table
and opening the grassy lawns to invasion by corn lilies and lodgepole pine.
The process was imperfectly understood, and the Park Service was not sure
what should be done about it.

Sumner and Grater offered Carl a National Park Service contract to do a
study. He was to try to ascertain the original condition of the meadows in
Sequoia-Kings Canyon National Park, assess the amount of damage that had
been done, and suggest means to return them to their original state.

Carl, too, was concerned about the meadows, but he didn't give an imme-
diate answer. It would be a difficult and complex job, and he had some
doubts as to how well his education suited him for it. He mulled the matter
over for some time before signing the contract and dropping it in the mail.
Actually, he was too modest. They couldn't have picked anyone more meticulous in method or more intent upon the welfare of the mountain environment.

Once committed, he threw himself into the effort to save the meadows he
loved so well. There was little time to read up on the subject as it was late
May by the time he made the decision, and he wanted to get into the field as
early as possible after the school year ended. First he searched the archives at
Sequoia-Kings to try to discover the condition of the meadows before the
incursions of man and pack animals. He learned that about fourteen years ear-

lier Lowell Sumner had made a series of meadow photographs. They were a godsend, for they gave him a base from which to make comparisons.

Although he hadn't owned a camera since his boyhood Brownie, Carl bought one and learned to use it. He felt insecure about his photography, but the pictures he took clearly illustrated his findings. Fortunately he could call on his range plant botany course at Pullman to help in understanding meadow growth, and he had, to some extent, studied the physical properties of soils. Now he must put it all together with his observations to see the history of meadows in perspective.

He determined to survey as many back country meadows as possible in order to have a broad basis for his study. There were logistic problems to solve in covering the vast country from Blaney Meadows in the northern extremity of Kings Canyon National Park all the way to the extreme south of Sequoia National Park, and from down in the woods up to treeline. He traveled most of the time on foot with a pack, occasionally by horseback, and once with saddlehorses, packer, and mule. He tried a burro but it walked too slowly, and he wore himself out walking behind the swinging tail switching it with a stick.

Though it was hard work, sometimes drudgery, he enjoyed exploring this other great Sierran park which he had seen as a young man, and known briefly in the summer of 1941. Besides revisiting old haunts, in his lonely treks he came to know intimately a new world of peaks and valleys.

And there were golden moments. One late afternoon in the Roaring River drainage of the Kings River he came to Williams Meadow. The air was still, the day like mellow wine. Sun was streaming through the trees, the grass was green as Ireland, and at the far end of the meadow shimmered a group of aspens. Carl could easily imagine mounted horsemen in glittering armor riding toward him out of the trees, and far in the distance a turreted castle. It was the most romantic meadow he had ever seen.

More soberly, he did find alarming differences between the meadows still untouched and those that had suffered the depredations of pack stock. When he wrote up his report after the end of the field season, he made stringent and far-reaching recommendations.

The Park Service was pleased by the breadth of Carl's study and his careful analysis of the situation. Now they had a documented, rational basis for implementing changes. And changes were made. Many heavily damaged meadows were closed to grazing, and in others, trails were rerouted to go around, not through, the most fragile areas. The Park Service hoped by these

means to restore the meadows to
their former beauty and save them as
part of the precious Sierra heritage
that belongs to all the people.

Meanwhile, Carl's parents, Marie
and Charles, had bought a small lot
in Tujunga north of Los Angeles in
the San Fernando Valley. They set to
work to make a new home. Charles
had finally retired, but Marie was still
a dynamo for work. She thought
nothing of getting up at five in the
morning to mix concrete for lining
the walks. The two laboriously
removed rocks from their lot on an
ancient alluvial fan high above a river
wash, then dug pits and brought in
soil to fill them. They planted fruit
trees, berry bushes, vegetables, and
in the far corner a pepper tree with
rabbit hutches and chickens under it.
In front of the house was a beautiful
flower garden.

*On Mount Lyell, 1954. Photo by Robert
Gottlieb.*

His parents always showed great affection for Carl. Marie had loved Helen
as a daughter and sorrowed when Carl's marriage ended. Now that he was
alone, she welcomed him home with greater warmth than ever. Each time he
arrived she clasped him in her arms saying, "The prodigal son has returned!"

However, Marie began to grow thin and discovered that she had cancer.
Charles was devastated. After almost sixty years of marriage he could hardly
imagine living without her. In confusion and anguish he called on Carl to
advise him as to whether or not she should have surgery. Carl was deeply
touched when his strong, authoritarian father turned to him as though he
were the son asking a parent's advice.

Although there seemed little hope, they decided on the operation. It was
not a success. Marie lingered a while, growing weaker all the time. When
some of her women friends visited her in the hospital, she at last opened up
and talked about her difficult childhood, demonstrating with gestures the
beating of the flax.

When his mother finally died on her birthday in June, 1959 at the age of eighty-four, Carl went down to her funeral. He was distressed when he went to view the body and found her face disguised by cosmetics. In anguish he threw himself upon her, but she was as hard and cold as mountain stone. He felt more alone than ever.

Within a month of Marie's death, Sumner and Grater came back and offered Carl a new contract to do a meadow study in Yosemite. He had found satisfaction in working in Sequoia-Kings, but this was a sad time for him. He felt overburdened and depressed. His father seemed unable to cope with life since Marie's passing, and Carl himself felt more like drawing in with this fresh grief than taking on a new challenge. Then he remembered the old German saying, *"Arbeit macht das Leben süss"* — work makes life sweet. He accepted the contract.

Beginning was more difficult than it had been in Sequoia. Ranger Emil Ernst had done a few studies back in 1948, but aside from these there were almost no historic photographs. And bad as conditions had been in Sequoia, its back country had been more efficiently patrolled than Yosemite's and had fine redwood drift fences to control wandering stock.

Again, Carl visited all the meadows. He was furnished such stock as he needed. For the northern section he had a saddle horse and pack mule which he wrangled himself. With characteristic frugality he lived on iron rations and drove himself hard. Now and then when he saw the smoke of a trail crew camp he welcomed the prospect of some good grub and fellowship.

It was customary to fence off certain areas of the backcountry as "tourist pasture" where parties could turn their horses loose. The one in Pate Valley was badly degraded and in terrible condition. Carl needed to find an ecologically equivalent, untouched meadow for comparison. Following the Morrison Creek Trail he spotted an opening deep down in the timber that seemed to be what he was seeking. He fixed its location in his mind and headed that way.

As he went down, down, down with his half-Arabian saddle horse and his mule, it grew hotter and hotter. He had brought a sack of grain for the horse in case there wasn't enough forage in the meadow, but the sack came loose, and he stopped to retie it. He was working with the gear when the mule bit a hole in the sack. Carl thrashed at the mule's head with a stick and grabbed at the leaking sack, but the mule won the contest and got most of the food.

When they finally reached the base of the descent, they saw a shady grove of oaks ahead and ambled sleepily toward it. Suddenly there was an explosion of yellow jackets. The animals took off like two blue streaks, pans rattling into the brush and Carl hanging on for dear life. When at last they slowed, he slid to the ground, gathered up his scattered gear, and they continued on their way dignified but shaken.

He soon found the little meadow. It was wonderfully beautiful with grasses up to his shoulder and rich greenery covering the many windfallen trees. He stayed for several days. While there, he saw a little rattlesnake trying to go up a sandy bank, first darting forward, then sliding back defeated, time and again.

"Poor little fellow," he thought, "I'll help him out." He found a forked stick and very gently nudged the reptile up the bank. He was convinced it turned and smiled at him before slithering away into the grass.

From Pate Valley he took a week-long trip up the Rodgers Canyon trail to Rodgers and Benson Lakes and back. On the return Carl and his horse and mule again descended into the heat of Pate Valley, plodding sleepily along as they approached the grove of oak trees. He leaned over to the little mare's ear and said softly, "Don't you remember those yellow jackets?" Bang! She bolted again.

Carl discovered other wonderful things. In Turner Meadow where people seldom go, he found quantities of blossoming sundew — a tiny carnivorous flower made famous by Darwin's studies. In Virginia Canyon he was thrilled by the luxuriant growth on the mineral-rich metamorphic soil. And in many places in the park he found that meadows formerly used by the park horses for fall grazing had recovered when left alone a few years. He realized that other almost-ruined meadows could recover if given the chance.

One stock meadow called East Meadow had been gutted by floods. A forty foot deep gully crossed it, and as Carl gazed at its banks he saw a remarkable thing. Layers of rich organic soil (actually peat) alternated with other layers with logs embedded in them, some hanging out into the eroded cut. It came to him that he was reading an illuminated manuscript, the story of the alternation of meadow and forest going back hundreds of seasons.

For years afterward he urged any geology students he met to go see East Meadow. Finally one of them, Spencer Wood, a doctoral candidate in geology at the California Institute of Technology, followed the suggestion. By carbon 14 dating of charcoal fragments, Wood found that the age of the revealed layers in the gully was about ten thousand years. He also discovered that about 1500 years ago a massive eruption from volcanoes east of the Sierra had left a layer of ash in the strata. And, as Carl had surmised, the area was sometimes covered with forest and sometimes with meadow through those hundreds of years. It impressed upon him the transitory quality of the scene we see today in Tuolumne Meadows— yet oddly, its great permanence as well. Though the meadows and forests play musical chairs with their boundaries, meadow and forest remain.

When he returned from this second season in the field, Carl worked all winter and through the following spring on the report. As summer, 1961, approached, he toiled to finish it. He filed his report on June 29th and drove to Yosemite the same day.

A new uniform had been decreed, produced by a company in Merced, and he picked up the uniform on the way. Arriving late in Yosemite Valley, he managed about four hours sleep on the ground. By then it was morning, and he donned the new outfit and rushed to the lodge to meet a group he was to conduct for a week around the High Sierra Loop. They returned the following Saturday afternoon. The next Sunday morning, he picked up a new group and started again.

This went on for six consecutive weeks with never a day off between trips. It was a rainy season, and walking wet day after day, he was often soaked to the bone. He hadn't bothered with a raincoat, and the flimsy synthetic uniform didn't keep him warm. He caught cold and began to cough. His condition grew worse until after the sixth week he could go on no longer. They clapped him in the hospital with pneumonia, stuffed him with antibiotics, and kept him in bed the rest of the summer.

As a result of Carl's meadow study, many new restrictions were imposed in Yosemite. Other factors also reduced meadow damage. It became more expensive to rent pack animals, and backpacking grew ever more popular. Thus many meadows have had a long breathing spell to revive. They can now be enjoyed in a far more natural state than when Carl began his studies.

24
Hoarded Treasure: The Herbarium

"Knowledge this man prizes best
Seems fantastic to the rest,
Pondering shadows, colors, clouds,
Grass-buds and caterpillar shrouds."
— Ralph Waldo Emerson

Winter and summer Carl kept himself busy. He loved the high mountains as steadfastly as ever — perhaps more, now that he had fewer close human ties. And he was as earnestly devoted as ever to his teaching. Yet there was a sense of emptiness he couldn't shake.

In 1946, his two chief passions came together as Carl proposed the creation of a herbarium that his students could use for reference at San Jose State. Dr. Carl D. Duncan, Head of the Department of Biological Sciences, favored the idea, and Carl set to work.

There was already a herbarium of sorts at the school, but when he looked it over, Carl shook his head in dismay. The specimens were mangled and poorly mounted, often mislabeled, and insects had had their way with them. He threw them all out, six cans full, and tromped them down with his feet in the trash container. Then he cleaned the cases and was ready to start.

He used the private collection he had been accumulating over the years as a core for the new collection. When the university built a new wing on the old Science Building, they gave him a room and more herbarium cases, and he set up a desk in the corner. Here he was to spend long hours poring over a microscope, mounting specimens, and studying the taxonomic literature.

In a big university herbarium like the one at Berkeley, much of the mounting and filing is done by assistants. Occasionally Carl had help — San Jose State was willing to pay for staff — but he quickly learned that as soon as he had trained someone to do the job, he or she moved on and he had to start all over with a new helper. As this was time consuming, Carl eventually settled for doing it all himself.

On mountain hikes and lowland excursions he amassed his peculiar harvest. In his tent in Tuolumne Meadows there was usually a large granite rock weighing down a bulging plant press. Gradually the word went out, and specimens began to arrive from far-away places: Texas, New England, Hawaii, Greenland, even Tonga. Roger McGehee, later a ranger-naturalist colleague at Tuolumne Meadows, sent plants from the southwest desert. A senior botany student named Jim once mailed in some Mexican specimens which arrived in poor condition. When Carl next met him, he casually asked, "Were the Mexicans friendly, Jim?"

John and Linnea, 1957.

"Yes, very."

"Well," Carl observed, "by the looks of your specimens, I thought the natives must have been chasing you with spears."

Exotic collections demand exotic reference material, and Carl found it a help when plants had been previously identified in the field. When they had not, he had to work out identifications from those books available. He gradually built up a library of taxonomic works, turning to second-hand sources for long out-of-print books, as well as keeping up with the latest publications in the field.

Once identified and mounted, the specimens had to be protected from the ever-voracious insects that prey on these academic treasures. At intervals, Carl chemically fumigated them.

The rage to name, to classify — what is it, anyway? "Many lovers of nature . . . do not feel that they are truly in touch with it until they have mastered the names of a great many flowers and trees," said Edward Sapir, "as though the primary world of reality were a verbal one and as though one could not get close to nature unless one first mastered the terminology which somehow magically expresses it."

No doubt for Carl the reality-creating function of language was part of it. Yet taxonomists express a great deal more in their labels and lists than mere identification. The name is a key to everything that is known about the plant, for it unlocks the literature. Through names, a botanist plucks the strings of creation and evolution — getting to know the intricate life stories of species, genera and families as part of the life story of the planet.

To Carl, bending over his dried pressed plants and examining through a microscope their delicate differences, this was never a museum of dead things. It was an assemblage of life. In the long hours at his desk he found that the plants were a solace, a companionship, a forgetting of the sorrows of this world, and working on them was a sweet labor. Gradually it absorbed all his spare time. As he fulfilled each day's responsibilities, he looked forward to his secret joy, his herbarium specimens. He no longer tried to grow flowers in his yard, he hurried through his simple household chores, he was absorbed.

On October 7, 1977, the herbarium was formally dedicated and named for Carl. Dr. Askell Love gave an address on alpine plants, and a bronze plaque commemorated the occasion. By this time, Carl had collected over thirteen thousand specimens in 1300 different genera — not remarkable compared to the extensive herbaria of great universities, but remarkable indeed for San Jose State. He was happy.

As he grew older, Carl's satisfaction deepened. "The herbarium — that's really something to leave behind me," he said to himself. Although not much given to speculating about death and immortality, he thought that the bronze plaque and the cases of carefully prepared specimens were the best kind of monument he could imagine.

Beyond the Sierra

Carl resting during hike in the Swiss Alps, 1986. Photo by Milt Irvine.

25
Switzerland Refound

"Every mountain now hath found a tongue,
And Jura answers, through her misty shroud,
Back to the joyous Alps, who call to her aloud!"
— Lord Byron

All his life Carl hoped to return one day to Switzerland, a country he could scarcely recall. He felt his roots were there.

As a child he spoke *Schwyzer Duutsch*, the Germanic language of Switzerland. In graduate school he studied German, and ever afterwards read German scientific papers and enjoyed the poetry of Goethe and other German writers. Then too, his father had corresponded faithfully with a wide circle of relatives in the old country, and Carl read the letters, which were written not in dialect but in High German. Thus he felt prepared, should the opportunity arise, to return to the old country as something of a native.

After Marie died, Charles Schaarschmidt revisited the land of his youth. It had changed much from the Switzerland he remembered. Though he enjoyed seeing it, he was content to return to California where, in 1969, he too passed away at the age of 95.

In 1974 the University of California at Berkeley asked Carl to lead a summer botanical trip to his almost-native land. He was excited at the prospect. At last he could return to Basel and see the Swiss Alps and alpine flowers he had dreamed of for so long.

Marsh Pitman, a junior college entymology teacher, was to be his assistant. Together they took a scouting trip before the rest of the group arrived. Carl was awed by the great peaks of the Berner Oberland, their huge masses of rock and ice rising above green valleys dotted with fine old chalets. It all seemed so civilized compared to the Sierra! One minute you could be sipping coffee and eating crusty rolls with butter and marmalade, and five minutes later be climbing mountains.

In his explorations, Carl boarded the mountain railroad which goes to the Jungfraujoch or high saddle of the Jungfrau, and got off at the Eiger Glacier Station to stay overnight. As he sat in the restaurant at the station listening to the barking mountain rescue dogs and to the waiters speaking their rich Berner dialect, he thought of his mother and smiled to himself. He was really in the Alps at last!

The next morning he poked about in the nearby meadows and discovered lovely skeins of *Dryas* or mountain avens spread over the ground like green fishnets full of creamy blossoms. On some ledges grew the *Schweizer Mannsschild* (Swiss Man's Shield) a kind of *Androsace* that hangs over rock walls in a bulbous cushion covered with white flowers. It was a real find. He made a note that it grew above the railroad track.

Finally his group arrived — 25 congenial people from all over the United States, some experts and some novices, ready to meet the alpine flowers in a dramatic high mountain setting. They based the first part of their three-week stay in Wilderswill just out of Interlaken.

The day came for their ride to the Jungfraujoch. Where the train pierces the limestone wall of the Eiger, it stopped. They could look through a window at the grim rock and ice of the infamous north face that has claimd so many lives.

At the Eiger Glacier Station on the trip down, Carl impulsively suggested that they get off and walk to Kleine Scheidegg, a high saddle some distance below the frowning Eiger and the serene Jungfrau. He was thinking of the *Schweizer Mannsschild*. Like the Pied Piper, he had only to speak and the group trooped behind, though a heavy mist enveloped them, and it began to rain.

He was following a ridge which seemed familiar. After going uphill for some time, he became confused. "You stay here and I'll check ahead," he told his cheerful shivering crew. While they waited in the mist and drizzle, he moved forward until he was staring over a cliff into a sea of fog. This couldn't be the route. Rejoining the others he took another tack, and after some time they came to a boulderfield rich in flowers. But where were the railroad tracks to guide him?

The rain kept falling. On and on they wandered down the slope. All this time they had been high above timberline, but eventually they descended to the first trees. Unknown to Carl, they had walked right over the track; it was covered with snow sheds built so long ago that they were entirely overgrown and indistinguishable from the rest of the terrain.

Far down the mountainside the mist lifted and they could see the cliffs bordering the Lauterbrunnen Valley, the wrong valley for them. Drenched brown cows were standing around a little herdsman's hut, and trails led off into the abyss. Continuing down slope they reached Wengen and caught the train back to Wilderswill where, after drying out, they dined in style and laughed about their adventure. Carl smiled and smoked and never admitted he had not known all along where they were going.

Another excursion was to Schynige Platte by cog railroad. On a mountain spur they visited the old botanical garden planned by Swiss botanist Karl Schröter. Here Professor Lüdi had studied the effect of overgrazing in the Alps. Cows, goats, and grasses have been living on this upland more or less harmoniously for thousands of years. The present flora represents plants that can coexist with livestock, yet their delicate balance is easily upset by overgrazing. Here the group saw the Nardus grass which flourishes in areas of diminishing mineral nutrition owing to too many farm animals. Even the picture-postcard Alps show the ruinous effects of pressure on the ecosystem.

One evening Carl sat playing his harmonica and watching the sunset from the Faulhorn above Grindelwald. As he played the old Swiss songs his parents had taught him, a couple sitting nearby were dumbfounded that an American should know so much of their traditional music, and invited him home to visit their farm.

From Wilderswill the Americans traveled by bus to the little old town of Meiringen, past the enormous Finsteraarhorn of gleaming glaciers, and over the Grimsel Pass. Carl was charmed to see the rock change from gray to granite-green as it became covered with map-lichen at the higher elevations.

Then down to grass-green slopes covered with paradise lilies, and a view of the Rhone Glacier hanging like an expiring white dragon on the mountainside. They could clearly trace the place, miles down the valley, where the receding glacier snout had rested over a century ago.

Next into the ancient Canton of Uri. In these deep valleys the walls are subject to terrible avalanches, and houses are built with thick stone avalanche shields on the uphill slope. Then over the Saint Gothard Pass to the Ticino or Italian Switzerland. They were discovering what a big little country Switzerland is. Crossing a corner of Italy, they reentered Switzerland and bused up to Maloja for another base, another round of mountain hikes and new flowers.

Carl relished the Swiss food, particularly breakfast with *Weckli* or rolls, fresh gruyère cheese, *Konfitüren* (preserves), and *Schale,* or half coffee/half milk.

Savoring their simple goodness he reflected on his father's old saying, "The Lord gave us food but the devil gave us cooks," and wondered how they could ruin food in the United States the way they do. He recalled the last time he had bought something called a Swedish coffee cake in San Jose. Why, he thought, you might as well take a spoon and eat out of a lard can!

After the three-week group trip ended he had the rest of the summer to himself. He went to Basel and stayed some time with his cousin Gretel, daughter of his glamorous Aunt Bertha. She welcomed him as a long-lost brother, though they had last met as very young children and hardly remembered each other. He was the returned one, the one who had somehow been faithful, who had remembered the language (though now and then he missed a word).

Carl was astonished by her all-encompassing religiosity. When he was growing up, he had passed through a period when he began to question the deeply held Calvinistic beliefs of his parents, and accepted a more scientific view of cosmology. But he had learned not to distress his family by saying anything, and so it was with Gretel. During the month he stayed with her he dutifully accompanied her to church and read the Bible with her. She was happy in his company.

One day they walked through a market fair where all was bustle and display, buying and selling, music and dancing. Gretel was alarmed. Surely the devil lurked at every corner! She seized his forefinger and almost dragged him through the crowd, looking neither right nor left, and not pausing until they reached home, when she knelt down on the doorstep and thanked God for bringing them back safely.

Carl wanted to see his mother's birthplace, and on a weekend he and Gretel went to the little village of Tschugg in the Canton Freiburg at the outlet of the Bielersee. He asked around if anyone could remember his mother's family, but no one recalled the name. The host of the village winehouse shrugged. "Bad times, those were bad times. They all went hungry, and many people left." In this green prosperous countryside, it was hard to think of famine no longer ago than his mother's childhood.

What a fine city Basel was, just as he had expected! He visited its great rosy-stoned cathedral and city hall, and listened to the drum and fife corps, marching and drumming in an intricate rhythm that only a Basler can master. As he walked about the streets he watched the children going to school with their little rucksacks of books, and began following people just to listen to their speech, so sweet to his ears. It was as though his parents had come back

Carl plays Alpenhorn, Sion, Switzerland, 1986. Photo by Milt Irvine.

and were talking to him. As if he were a boy again.

In the Basler Kunstmuseum, Carl responded to the beauty and intensity of the Cranach paintings. And he was deeply moved by the Holbein portraits of Luther and Erasmus, two sides of the coin of European culture, and both sides heads.

In 1978, four years after this memorable trip, Carl had the chance to visit Switzerland again. This time the university asked if he would like to choose his assistant, and he picked Will Neely, his friend of many years from Tuolumne Meadows. Many of the same people who had accompanied Carl in 1974 came along to revive old acquaintances among the flowers, and to find some new ones.

This time at the Eiger Wall the ice was breaking off and clattering down. Some time earlier some climbers had fallen on the north wall, and one body still hung from the cliff because it was too dangerous to bring him down. The hard face of the Alps showed briefly in this dreadful incident. Carl shuddered. "This is a world of certain death," he said.

When they reached the Jungfraujoch it was snowing hard. He climbed above the restaurant to the saddle, thinking about how the first Everest climbers had used it as a training ground. In the driving snow he could imagine he was in the Himalaya.

They took an aerial tramway high above Grindelwald and hiked across a rolling upland to Grosse Scheidegg, a saddle on the opposite side of the valley from the Kleine Scheidegg where Carl had his adventure four years earlier. Winter lingered in the hollows, and the fringed purple soldanella pushed up through little holes in the snow. After lunch, Carl noticed that the town of Meiringen was far below them on the lake. Ignoring the tremendous distance, he started down the trail and had to be strenuously dissuaded from leading the group on another quixotic ramble. Seventy-six years old, he had never lost the ardent enthusiasm of youth.

As the day grew late, they rushed back toward Grindelwald. On the way down Carl noticed a *Biscutella*, a plant in the mustard family he had never seen, but knew about because of genetic studies done on it long ago. He wanted desperately to stop, admire, and collect a specimen, but as with so many travelers on so many voyages, the passing glimpse was all he could seize, and the scene disappeared like a phantom in his mind.

From Maloja they visited the Forno Glacier and found a beautiful yellow saxifrage with red spots (*Saxifraga aizoides*), along with other new plants. They searched everywhere for edelweiss but it kept eluding them. Finally down in the Val dal Fain in a level pasture full of grazing cows, they discovered a big patch of the famous woolly white flower that everyone loves.

One of Carl's relatives was in the Swiss Army, and when Carl saw his army pack he began to want one like it. To his disappointment, sale of this military item was not permitted. However, in an antique store Will Neely found him an old one made all of skins with the fur on the outside to shed water and snow.

When the trip was over and he said goodby to Will, he thought with nostalgia and affection of their long years of friendship as blood-brothers in the mountains. Neither foresaw that this was the last time they would be together on the trail. Will suffered from increasing ill health, and died in 1985.

Carl went on to Zermatt and stayed in the Hotel Monte Rosa with its plaque commemorating Edward Whymper, the famous, tragic Englishman who made the first ascent of the Matterhorn. Whymper never recovered from the anguish of seeing four of his party of seven fall to their deaths on the descent from the summit. In the little graveyard by the river Carl walked among the tombstones, some with an ice axe and a coil of climbing rope carved upon the face, reliving the sorrow for so many young climbers who had come here in the pride of their youth and had remained forever.

Climbing can be a cruel pursuit. But even Carl's own quiet calling of botany has its martyrs. Students of the great Linnaeus went all over the world collecting, and many died young of tropical diseases and accidents in far away lonely places. Their names are perpetuated in the names of the flowers.

He visited Gretel again and she greeted him as warmly as before. This time, at Carl's insistence, they went to the famous Rigi, a very strange ancient geological formation. The whole mountain looks as if covered with cobbles, and is named Nägelfluhberg or Mass-of-Nails Mountain.

Then they went to Goldau. He had read about how, a hundred years ago, the entire top stratum of the mountain slid off and buried a nearby village. Gretel first learned of this tragedy from visiting the site with Carl.

Back in Basel, he visited the Swiss Pharmaceutical-Historical Museum and met the custodian. She graciously took him along ancient creaky floors through a sixteenth century apothecary's laboratory with everything in place. It seemed as though it should have been draped in cobwebs and guarded by bats. Carl was thrilled to learn that in this very laboratory "that rascal Paracelsus" (the alchemist Theophrastus Bombastus von Hohenheim) worked for years until the burghers of Basel ran him out of the country. Finally they went into a locked room containing shelves of original fifteenth century herbals, and both leaned reverently over the beautiful ancient drawings.

During the journey, Carl had collected many plant specimens. He was concerned to get them safely home. His cousin made arrangements through the botany department of the University of Basel, and the plants were waiting when he returned to San Jose — a precious treasure for his beloved herbarium.

His journey into the past was not yet over. He went on to London for a couple of weeks and found a room in a cheap hotel. It was awful — cold, damp, and high-ceilinged, with a gas jet no longer in use and a grimy window opening onto a courtyard full of miserable weeds. The room drove him to get out early and stay away until late.

He walked the streets he had known as a boy, saw the changing of the guard at Buckingham Palace, visited Westminster Abbey and stood with moist eyes as he copied the inscriptions in the poets' corner. Outside he recalled walking under the damp mossy arches so long ago. He went down to Greenwich to see the location of the prime meridian, viewed the Boadicea

Monument and Cleopatra's Needle, and strolled the Thames embankment.

Along the embankment he stopped to watch a man doing fine crayon drawings on the sidewalk. "These are beautiful," Carl told him. "You're the first screever I've seen."

"Yes, there aren't many of us left," agreed the old man. Carl dropped a coin in his cap.

"Thank you, sir. God bless you, sir," said the screever.

Carl had wanted as a boy to go to Madam Tussaude's Wax-Works. But there was something called a Chamber of Horrors, and his mother forbade it. Now at last he could see it.

He passed the London hospital where he had been sick with diphtheria in 1911, and the house on Saint Pancras Street in a neighborhood no longer a slum. The custodian told him an old woman who didn't like to be disturbed lived in his family's former flat. So he contented himself with looking up at the lantern where he and Gus had roasted potatoes and chestnuts in a faraway time. For a moment it seemed only yesterday.

At Kew he visited the herbarium and met a fellow taxonomist working on some of the early collections from India. How wonderful, Carl thought, to have botanical treasures from the whole world to study!

Everywhere he went he heard Cockney. "Where can I hear some good English?" he wondered. Then he saw an advertisement for Shaw's *Pygmalion,* bought a ticket, and spent an evening reviving his faith in the language.

On the homeward flight he had a seat by the window and glued his eyes to the scene below. At first there was just ocean. Then icebergs in blue water, then the fjords of Greenland with tongues of ice like frozen rivers flowing down them. He could see Greenland's strange form, mountains rimming the coast and the interior a great high saucer filled with a vast sea of ice seven to ten thousand feet thick. As they flow from the interior the glaciers crowd between the peaks, reaching speeds of two hundred feet a day on their rush toward the sea.

As he stared in wonder and awe, he was interrupted by a flight attendant. "Please close your curtain, sir. The movie is about to start." He fumed inwardly, closed the curtain, and found another spot where he could squeeze against a little peephole and continue his enraptured contemplation.

Over Canada he could clearly see the bare Laurentian Shield streaked with Protozoic and Cambrian rocks, and the glacier-formed lakes running north and south, bordered by eskers or narrow ridges that go for miles and miles.

Then a few trees that grew thicker until the land was covered with dense spruce forest as far as the eye could see. As they droned westward, specklings of autumn color appeared. At last the jumbo jet came down in Chicago and disgorged its load of people who had eaten and drunk and watched a movie, while Carl had been surveying the history of the earth.

Eight long years later, in 1986, Carl returned a third time to the land of his birth. A number of his friends organized a trip to be led jointly by Carl and Peter Steiger, a young Swiss student of landscape architecture who had worked as a volunteer in Tuolumne Meadows.

Peter was full of enthusiasm for his own mountains of Switzerland. He devised a three-week itinerary that enabled the visitors to see a great variety of the uncommon as well as the common plants. And although they traveled by train and bus and boat to remote spots, so efficient are the Swiss schedules, and so thorough was Peter's planning, that they never had to wait more than ten minutes for the next ride.

The eighteen people saw about three hundred different plants in their three weeks. Carl had not realized before how many areas of endemism there are in Switzerland — places where plants occur that are found nowhere else.

One notable area was the mountain called La Grigna, near Lecco on the Lago di Como. Here they found a strange sedge with a snow-white perigynea, an unusual buttercup with huge blossom and leathery leaves, and *Kernera*, a member of the mustard family growing in crevices of the limestone.

Near Sion in the Rhone Valley was a special grass, a *Stipa*, with plumes fifteen centimeters long, and the Swiss *Ephedra*, close cousin of our western mormon tea. And in the Swiss National Park, the alpine meadow-rue which has only been found in one location in the Sierra. It's a precious two-inch edition of the common three-foot tall plant familiar on Sierra slopes.

After the group trip ended, Carl rented a room on the Wallensee, a quiet place to stay a while before joining Gretel. He had only been there a day or two when Toni and Richard Corelli arrived to take him touring with them in a rented car. The three set off together to explore the countryside, playing Mozart tapes as they rolled along.

There's a peak in Switzerland called the Grosse Mythen which is a piece of the African continent that was pushed up into Switzerland sixty million years ago. Carl had longed to see it, and now they took a cable car to the top and he was able to explore it. He was ecstatic.

For the third time that he could remember, he celebrated the Swiss National Holiday on August 1st — an occasion like our Fourth of July, full of merriment and solemn thoughts.

They drove up the Lauterbrunnen Valley with its Yosemite-like waterfalls and stayed in the tiny village of Stechelberg. In his room above a bakery, Carl woke at daybreak to smell the fresh-baked bread. What a joy! At breakfast he told Toni and Richard, "Most of the bread in America is a travesty of the Lord's wheat!"

From the town of Gandria on Lake Lugano, they took a cable car to the top of Monte Bre and hiked back down while Carl recited Kipling. Wild cyclamen were blooming in profusion, and there were many Ostrya trees. One of these furnished him wood to carve a walking stick.

Chairlifts were another matter. In the Dolomites he had his first chairlift ride — and fell fast asleep. When Toni and Richard noticed, they whooped and shouted to wake him up in time to get off. Later a snowstorm over-whelmed them, with thunder and lightning and fog. The three of them found their way to a hut where, alpine style, the owner was serving nourish-ing minestrone. Not like the Sierra, where you're really on your own. When the sun came out again, they emerged to a winter wonderland in summer and had a snowball fight.

Carl found these jaunts a bit fatiguing but wonderfully exciting, and was ever a good companion. He nibbled wild edible fruits and mushrooms like a boy let out of school, told stories, sang songs, recited poetry, and sometimes even danced a jig. What matter that his arthritis sometimes nagged, and sometimes the weather was wet?

Yet all good things come to an end. A long wait in the Paris airport, a mid-night arrival in New York, two hours sleep and another long flight. And at last he was back in the little house in San Jose, rich in memories, rich in new plants for the herbarium, and glad to be home.

26

Further Afield—Mexico, Alaska, the Colorado Rockies

arl's enduring and absorbing focus has been on the alpine botany of the Sierra Nevada. In Washington State and Minnesota, although he collected and studied the local flora, his mind was ever on the California mountains.

Nevertheless, he had a lifelong interest in all the floras of the world. He spent hours over books and reports of exotic lands, though he visited them only in dreams. Actually, he had traveled little since his boyhood wanderings with his family. Then, starting in the nineteen seventies, he began to explore more widely and to meet new floras.

In the spring of 1971, even before his first trip to Switzerland, three of his students arranged a camping trip into Mexico and prevailed on him to go along. They would pay for the gas and do the cooking, and Carl could study, collect, and teach.

He took with him Shreve and Wiggins's recently published *Vegetation and Flora of the Sonoran Desert*. It contains an excellent discussion of the physical features of the great natural area he was about to visit, its perennial and ephemeral plants, and the ecology of various species.

As they drove south, Carl came under the spell of the desert, remembering its magic from the days of the Coconino Trips with the Trailfinders. In some ways, he realized, desert plants are like alpines. They have evolved strategies for living in extremes that most temperate zone plants cannot tolerate. Sierra plants face cold, dryness, wind, and solar radiation. The desert also experiences great daily variations in temperature, though not the bitter cold of alpine regions. Winds dry and heat burns, and at times there are engulfing floods. A desert plant must be able to survive all of these.

As John C. Van Dyke said seventy years before, "Nature has other animals beside man to look after, other uses for her products than supporting human life. She toils and spins for all alike and man is not her special care. The desert

vegetation answers her purposes, and who shall say her purposes have ever
been other than wise?"

Carl saw the tough and wily desert perennials that blossom opportunisti-
cally when a little rain makes the desert into a flower garden, and go into a
kind of hibernation when rains are withheld. He found annuals that spring up
almost overnight, blossom and fruit in a reproductive fury, then shed their
seeds and die before the relentless dry season can destroy them. The seeds,
too, are cunning in their genes; they can lie about for years if the weather is
unpropitious, to sprout anew and start the cycle again at a touch of moisture.
In this mysterious ecosystem, wax-skinned swollen cacti hoard their moisture
inwardly, protecting it from marauders with vicious spines. Alongside a fierce
barrel cactus Carl might find a seemingly defenseless little desert marigold.
But he could see its wonderful coating of white hairs that reflect rather than
absorb the rays of the sun, and thus prevent disastrous loss of water.

Some plants were bristly, some hairy, some succulent and swollen — all
features found in alpine species. Yet desert plants have a dazzling variety of
other adaptations. He delighted in those with sap as thick as honey, slow to
evaporate in the heat, and in those that concentrate in their tissues alkaloids
and other animal-repellent chemical compounds. Perhaps the most notable
was the sacred datura, close relative of eastern North America's jimson weed,
with massy evil-smelling leaves and a majestic trumpet of pale lavender. Carl
knew that to the Indians it was sacred for the visions it could bring, yet fearful
(as the sacred often is) because of the madness and death which attend its
misuse.

In a way, he found the desert like the sacred datura, a fearful and beautiful
region to be approached with veneration and circumspection.

He and his companions drove south through Nogales and Guaymas and
camped in the beneficent desert sunshine near Hermosillo. In the rich thorn
forest they found the morning glory tree, graceful, gray-limbed, and covered
with white blossoms. Mexicans call it *palo blanco*, the white tree, or sometimes *palo del muerto*, deadman's tree — again, the intimate connection of
beauty and death.

Carl had long known the ocotillo of the California and Arizona deserts, its
slender arching stems laden with scarlet blossoms. Now he was to meet its
unusual red-bloomed relative, *palo Adán* or Adam's tree, with a thick twisted
trunk sometimes ten inches through.

The boys took him to Bahia Kino where pale-sanded desert meets the
benign blue waters of the Sea of Cortez. How different it all was from the

alpine land he knew, yet, like it, beautiful and spare.

Cookery was a mystery to his companions, and Carl began to suffer from a diet of hard-boiled eggs and crackers. On the return trip he provided himself with a supply of sweet buns from a *panadería*, but one night the boys finished them off after he had gone to sleep, and he was back to hard-boiled eggs.

After a week he returned with a pile of specimens — *Abutilons* and other members of the Mallow family, many beautiful grasses, Cassias, Acacias, and others. The trip had only whetted his appetite for Mexico, and he hoped to return.

Not long after, he made a second foray south of the border, a brief one, to Desambuque, a Seri Indian village on the west coast facing the Sea of Cortez, opposite the Island of Tiburón. Carl enjoyed these peaceful and very poor people who had only recently given up their warlike rejection of the Mexicans, and now sold beautiful ironwood carvings. Unfortunately, he had very little time to collect plants.

Annetta Carter, who had been a close friend to both Carl and Helen for many years, urged him to visit her house in Loreto on the east coast of Baja California. In late November, 1974, he had a chance to go there with a group of other botanists.

Annetta had become an authority on the flora of Baja California and had published a number of papers describing new species of the region. Her simple house was on a little lot on the outskirts of Loreto, with a palm-thatched ramada in the back sheltering a table and a fireplace with stone slab for making tortillas.

She arranged to take the group into the nearby Sierra de la Giganta. They drove far up a canyon to a rancho where they rented burros to take them farther back into the Arroyo Gavilán. Remembering the feisty burros he had seen in the Sierra, Carl was impressed by the docility of these, the tremendous loads they carried, and their agility and speed.

At the head of the canyon, they found water to camp by. Huge Palmer's figs plastered themselves against vertical cliffs, their white knotty roots flowing down like water. The following day, the group climbed to the divide between Cerro Gavilán and Cerro Teombó, having come all the way from the low desert into the oaks. Mexico is a land of marvellous oak trees, twice as many species as in the United States, and Carl collected specimens from as many as he could. Near the top of the divide he found a rare wild cucumber and a little spring surrounded by huge Liebmann's oaks.

The group went on, but Carl felt like a child in a candy shop — so much to see! He remained behind to collect and found some remarkable things: a member of the Dogbane family with a fine delicate tapering stem topped by a flower, a tiny-leaved odorous *Bursera* or copal, and tropical mistletoe with big scarlet blossoms. On the way down he discovered a beautiful figwort, a family which has many representatives in the mountains of California. When he returned to camp, the backs of his hands were bloody from spines and stickers, and his palms smelled of incense from the scented copal.

On this trip he collected several *Jatrophas*, strange varied tropical shrubs in the drought-loving *Euphorbia* family. He found six different copals and four relatives of the ocotillo including the majestic white-flowered species occurring only in Baja California.

Visiting Loreto another year, Carl, Annetta, and their companions took a boat to Isla Carmen. He knew there was a native wild cotton that grew only on this island, and he collected a specimen. This seemingly barren island holds rich treasures for the trained botanist or zoologist. However, their boatman said a storm was blowing up, and they left in a hurry.

As they pitched and lurched in the wind, they feared the flimsy little craft would ship water and founder. But the pilot steered them into a sheltered harbor where all was calm, waiting until the storm passed to return to the mainland.

The plant world south of the border was strange and absorbing. Carl savored his Mexican experiences. Yet, appreciating desert and tropic, he hankered after the far northlands which hovered always in his mind. He longed to see the shimmering cotton grass, cloudberry, dwarf spruce, and other arctic species from which many of the alpines derived. He felt that he knew them well, although most he had glimpsed only in herbarium cases. In 1981, in his seventy-eighth year, it was given to him to see them in their native land.

He was invited to accompany an Alaskan trip sponsored by the University of California at Santa Cruz. The university did the advertising, arranged for lodging, and furnished an assistant. As in Europe, Carl's job was simply to revel and teach, to lend his eyes, his knowledge, and his enthusiasm to others.

When the assistant materialized, Carl was as enchanted as if he'd come upon a new lupine. Twenty-one year old Fiona Wilson, "the prettiest girl you ever saw," was to do the chores and look after him, arrange for buses and see to the luggage, and make the trip memorable with her boundless energy and versatility. From San Jose, she and Carl and another couple set out by car for Seattle.

In Portland, he asked to drive around a bit while he remembered a chapter of his boyhood. He hoped to find the site of his parents' restaurant, but everything was different. Even the Morrison Street Bridge was no more.

The ferry from Seattle was an ugly, ungainly boat. They were shown to the rear deck where swarms of young people, many with children and all with camping gear, were setting up housekeeping and cooking meals. Carl threw his sleeping bag down on the deck with the others.

The ferry took the inland passage, stopped at Ketchikan and Petersburg, then on to Juneau. He was fascinated watching the Canadian and Alaskan coast slide by to starboard, somber forests coming down to the sea, dark green islands looming on the port side, sparkle of water, cry of seabirds, and a long white wake behind.

Fiona amused herself playing hacky-sack on deck with the boys. Carl sat on his sleeping bag, smoked his pipe, and reread John Muir's accounts of his Alaska travels. Now and then the door opened and some stout gentlemen with cigars came out to see how the other half lived.

They landed at Juneau and went on to Glacier Bay. With two weeks' lead-time, they set up camp and began exploring.

Two rangers took Carl on a three day trip to see the glaciers. They boarded a ship named Nunatak, transferred to a smaller boat, called Arête, and finally took to kayaks to explore High Miller Inlet, where they set up camp and hiked to a high ridge. It was rough going. They didn't get back until 2:00 A.M. of the long arctic day. Miles of the soft turf were covered with snow-white *Dryas octopetala*, the rose-like avens he had seen in Switzerland.

The next day they cruised around in the Arête. The rangers fished, tugging a big halibut aboard. On the North Gilbert Peninsula Carl botanized in luxurious wildflower gardens, content as a browsing deer. When he came back aboard, the ship chugged on. About noon they came to the Hopkins Glacier, feeling their way between small fragments of icebergs that everywhere littered the head of the inlet. Clad in dazzling white, the peaks beyond towered up like the Alps. At intervals the explorers heard a rumbling boom, an ice-fall from the glacier front calving icebergs.

As they kept moving, the Grand Pacific Glacier came into view, its upper reaches forming a wide and level expanse of white. A portion of its wall collapsed and made waves that rocked their little craft wildly. They had to anchor to a berg to keep from drifting too fast in the chilling glacial wind, and gazed up at a pinnacle of ice which seemed about to fall. As they cruised toward the opposite shore, winds kicking up three foot waves prevented their landing in the kayaks.

On a shore below the Reid Glacier they found calm water and a place to camp. It reminded Carl of Muir's passage, "To dine with a glacier on a sunny day is a glorious thing and makes common feasts of meat and wine ridiculous. The glacier eats hills and eats sunbeams." Sure enough, beside the glacier he observed that turfs of the mountain avens were pushed to one side by lateral movement of the devouring ice.

He still had time for more plant-browsing before his group arrived. Hearing of a bog where there were remarkable things growing, he went out to see for himself. It was splendid. The flora all seemed familiar. He could recognize a plant's genus immediately, having worked with these same families from the temperate and arctic-alpine zones for so long, but the species was often new.

On July 2nd he wrote, "glorious walk east up border of Bartlett Cove Lagoon to Bartlett River, heavy rain during the whole trip." He counted two hundred rings in several sections of large spruce logs cut to clear the trail — about the age of the forest in this place. The broad, lagoon-like river shimmered silver against long dark sweeps of forest, and he heard not a sound, nor saw a single mark of man. "Long may it remain so!" Then he added, "I arrived wet, wet, wet, about 6 P.M., at my welcome shelter."

When the group came, many were old friends. Some had been in Switzerland with him, some in the High Sierra, and there was even a couple he had known in graduate school. Some of them camped with him, and others stayed in the nearby hotel. For the campers the logistics weren't always easy. It rained, and keeping gear dry and spirits bright was something of a challenge. Carl floated above the petty frustrations, buoyed up by this pilgrimage to the mecca of alpine botanists, the circumpolar world.

He took the students to the wonderful bog. It was a treasure house of ferns, dwarfed white spruces comfortable in the intensely acid soil, and Sitka spruce with its fragrant bark covered by mosses and lichens. He met his first cloudberry, a lucent pale yellow, and a native crab apple. There was the giant Pacific skunk cabbage from over the sea in Asia, with leaves shoulder-high and a meter across, and two species of sundew, the insectivorous plant dear to Darwin which Carl had once found in Turner Meadow in Yosemite. The *Kalmia* or laurel here was tall and lanky, unlike its High Sierran cousin, but

just as pink and starry. It was named
for Peter Kalm, one of the impassioned and unfortunate young naturalists sent out by Linnaeus to leave
their bones in foreign soil and their
names in botany books. Carl was
reaching out to Siberia, to
Scandinavia, to Greenland as he met
the northern flora.

Oh, glorious bog stuffed with
Andromedas, rustling with *Kalmia,*
lighted with orchids which drove
their orchid expert to her knees in
ecstasy and mud! The white "shy
maidens"! And devil's club, reviled
for its thorns, was to him a wonder
of enormous palmate leaves catching
the light like church windows of
delirious green.

Carl and Old Man Cactus (Lophocereus
schotti), *1975. Photo by Grace Mason.*

At Glacier Bay the glacier has
been receding for the last two hundred fifty years. In this great laboratory
William S. Cooper, whom Carl had known at Minnesota, worked on his theories of plant succession. As the glacier melted, plants sprang up behind it.
Carl could see the first willow herbs and seedling spruce at the upper end
braving the cold breath and shifting sands of the glacier's snout. Below them
grow successively higher plants until finally they become a full fine forest at
the lower end of the bay.

Carl had been stimulated, too, by the work of Frederick E. Clements, for
many years the most noted plant ecologist. Clements thought that all plant
communities go through a succession of forms and eventually reach a climax,
a harmonious association of species which, if undisturbed by climatic changes
or other interruptions, will remain in equilibrium indefinitely. It has since
been shown that this is not always so, for some floras (notably in the Scottish
highlands) go through a circular succession where the supposed climax seems
to collapse and the entire cycle starts again.

Carl knew there is much more to learn of these matters. The history of our
changing views of nature's intricate dance of the species went through his
mind at Glacier Bay. For him it was a vast museum of life springing up after

cold glacial death, a wonderful form of resurrection.

Reveling in the arctic plants, he was amazed at their profusion. In the Sierra many of these same plants are found, but they are rare. *Crepis nana,* a little golden hawksbeard, has only five known locations in the entire Sierra. He felt disoriented, even a little exasperated, to find whole rich turfs of it on islets in the braided streams. It seemed to make nature a spendthrift.

The braided streams were a wonder in themselves. They rise from glaciers and run north into the Yukon — as Robert W. Service said, "Where the rivers all flow God knows where." Only at the lower end of Denali National Park is the drainage south toward Cook Inlet and Anchorage.

When the trip ended, some of the party stayed behind for several days in a cabin above Wonder Lake just outside the far end of Denali National Park. They spent the days feasting on blueberry pies and botany. Then everyone went home, leaving Carl and Fiona behind. He wanted very much to linger longer and fill out his growing plant collection. Happily, Fiona found a back-country ranger who agreed to let them use his cabin on the Sanctuary River in the Park.

The two of them stayed for a month in the little spruce log cabin with a wood stove and a pile of wood. Fiona insisted on doing much of the work. When she was splitting spruce he warned her, "Now, Fiona, don't reach too far or you'll hit the handle. The ranger's shed is probably full of broken handles."

He reckoned without her spirit. She gave him a furious look. "Now you leave me alone!" and went to chopping as hard as she could.

She picked blueberries and day after day constructed sourdough breads and blueberry muffins and pies. "Taste that," she would say, "and I want no complaints." He had no complaints; he couldn't have been happier.

The only thing he might have wished for was less humidity. In the damp cabin, washed clothes took forever to dry, and plant specimens never seemed to dessicate properly at all. He kept changing the blotters in his plant press and hoping for the best.

When he finally returned to San Jose with two hundred specimens, many had developed a little mold. He had to spend long hours with a tiny paint brush carefully flicking off the mold under a microscope. As he worked, he thought about the history of plant collecting. It had to have been invented in Europe, where the plants are delicate and dry easily. They fit, too, in the standard size plant press. What would he have done in the tropics, where some of the vines are three hundred feet long, and others so thick they just won't dry gracefully?

His care brought good results. He saved every one of the two hundred Alaskan plants to add to the herbarium.

At the end of the trip, Carl learned that Fiona had not been paid for her work as his assistant. Reflecting that he didn't really need all of his fourteen hundred dollar honorarium, he split it with her, with heartfelt thanks.

The Alaska trip was a culmination of Carl's studies of alpine flora. He had been to the cradle, the place where many of his dearest flower friends had had their origin, had met their aunts and uncles and cousins, and had come to understand their families better than ever before. He returned to Tuolumne Meadows rich in memories and deeper in knowledge: seventy-eight years old, and still learning.

Carl had now seen the flora of the Alps and the Arctic. But in all these years, he had never botanized in the American Rockies, richest center of alpine flowers within the continental United States.

As a student he had been aware of the great importance of the Rockies, where the first North American studies of arctic-alpine flora had been undertaken by Theodore Holm. Holm had previously worked on the arctic flora of Greenland. The University of Colorado has his fine collection. Yet it had never occurred to Carl to shift to the Rockies for his own work. The Sierra Nevada was too much a part of him. Rather, he applied the findings of other scholars in other places to the special conditions of the Sierra.

In the early summer of 1983 some of his devotees organized informally to take him to Colorado. He was delighted. Once again he had about twenty people with him, most of them old friends. They went to Rocky Mountain National Park and Estes Park, the Mount Evans area, over the Trail Ridge Road, and finally to Aspen.

When they arrived in Rocky Mountain National Park, they were met by Betty Willard, co-author with Ann Zwinger of *Land Above the Trees*, and an excellent guide to the high country. Years before, Carl had known Betty in the Yosemite Field School. Perhaps it was there that she developed her interest in alpine plant ecology. Later she studied in Europe, where the field has been dominated for years by the ideas of Braun-Blanquet of the University of Montpelier in France. He coined the term "plant sociology" for his elaborate method of studying plant communities. With this method, a student determines the relative frequency of various species in a given environment, and then studies the environment, its temperature, soil, daylight, and other characteristics. Thus ecological units can be established in terms of both habitat and inhabitants.

Betty Willard used Braun-Blanquet's approach in doing her doctoral dissertation, and later in *Land Above the Trees*. Now in Colorado she shared her knowledge in the field with Carl and his friends.

He was aware that most of the country above timerline is not, strictly speaking, tundra. Tundra is wet ground underlain by permanently frozen ground. In the summer it becomes marshy with standing pools of water and tufts of vegetation. In one spot only did he find true tundra and the arctic grass *Phippsia algida* which is associated with it. Though he had searched in Alaska, this was the first time he had encountered it.

During the Pleistocene the glaciation in the Rockies was almost continuous, with a relatively unbroken lane of tundra climate on its periphery. This allowed the migration of many more arctic plants than in the Pacific Coast mountain system where glaciation was broken up and separated. Thus in the Rockies fewer of the arctic-alpines have been lost, and the number of plant species above timberline is very great.

One of the alpine plant mysteries whose unraveling fascinated Carl concerned the *Podistera*, a tiny member of the Parsley family that grows on Sierran mountain slopes and tops. For many years it was known only there. Later it was also found in the White Mountains of California. It seemed to be the single species in its genus, but that didn't make sense geographically or taxonomically. Genera with only a single species are typically very old, and all their species but one have become extinct. Alpine floras, on the other hand, are relatively recent geologically and are composed of genera with related species in neighboring ranges. Where were the relatives *Podistera* should by rights have had?

Two botanists whom Carl had known at Berkeley, Lincoln Constance and Mildred Matthias, began working on the Parsley family and found there was a plant in the Colorado Rockies that resembled *Podistera* but had been put into another genus. In Alaska was another. Constance and Matthias finally determined that all three were *Podisteras*, distributed in the expected manner for alpine plants in western North America. They had solved the puzzle.

Carl never found the Alaskan *Podistera*, but he did find the one in Colorado, and could greet it as someone he had longed to meet.

Also in Colorado was avens or *Dryas*, the same species as in the Alps and Alaska, but here butter-yellow. He looked for snow willow but it refused to show itself — a small disappointment demonstrating that the search can be endless. One never comes to the last page. In this there is a kind of security, for a taxonomist will meet new adventure wherever he goes — perhaps even when he is poking about among the celestial ranges on the other side.

Carl was thrilled with the Trail Ridge Road which climbs to twelve thousand feet where the continent thrusts up in vast rolls of dark rock covered with alpine fellfields. A happy hunting ground.

One of his most precious possessions is his plant press, constructed long ago of two sturdy boards and a heavy strap. It goes with him everywhere, empty at the beginning of a journey and bulging with precious loot by the end of it. He almost lost it in Colorado.

On this particular day, he and the St. Goars had started down a beautiful valley to a lake they had heard about. Shortly they left the trail for a shortcut. Suddenly Carl stopped. "My plant press, where is it?"

He anxiously started to retrace his steps. Faster and faster downhill across a rocky moraine, he skipped like a mountain goat from rock to rock and never stopped long enough to test his footing. His somewhat younger companions panted behind, marveling at the agility of this octogenarian. When they finally found the press intact by the trail, Carl was supremely happy.

The last part of their trip was in Aspen, where opera was added to scenery. In a huge huge tent they heard the music to Verdi's *Falstaff,* the singers accompanied by a ninety-three piece orchestra.

Many a morning at breakfast in the hotel, Carl took turns with his friends reciting poetry, usually Shakespeare. He had a whole luxurious apartment to himself with several rooms where he could spread out his plants to dry. He felt a little uncomfortable with all this luxury. "It's fun once in a while," he concluded, "but you'd get awfully tired of it. You have a feeling you're getting out of touch with mother earth. It isn't natural." He asked himself, "How can people face life and death in the cities?" The thought turned him cold.

Carl had traveled far, and all roads led back to the Sierra. Each time he returned to Tuolumne Meadows, he felt a deep satisfaction. He understood that to know a single flora well depends upon long and intimate experience, not on the quick and superficial overview taken on the run. The California mountains had given him the long view. He was grateful for his myriad summers in their high alpine world.

Fruiting

Helen in 1966.

27
Helen, The End of the Trail

"Like as the waves make toward the pebbled shore,
So do our minutes hasten to their end."
— William Shakespeare

C arl felt, as the years passed, an unwavering loyalty and affection for Helen. Although their lives diverged, they intersected, too. He visited her when he could, and their mutual interest in John and Linnea bound them together.

Helen pursued her career vigorously, and was active in the Sierra Club and the California Native Plant Society. At the herbarium in Berkeley she answered queries for the Poison Control Center and helped put together a booklet on poisonous plants. She managed the plant exchange program, did some work for the Scott Lawn Company, and found time to publish a number of short papers in *Madroño* and the *Sierra Club Yodeler*. A shy person, she seemed to blossom in the outdoors leading botany hikes and short backpacks, and enjoyed a wide circle of friends. Carl sensed that she valued her freedom and made the most of it.

She and Annetta Carter continued to be close friends and collaborators, and often went on camping trips together. Helen visited her in Baja California on a number of occasions, beginning in 1961 when Annetta was building her little house in Loreto. Helen studied Spanish and entered joyously into the new culture and new natural scene. The two indomitable women went plant-hunting far into the back country, bumping along terrible washboard roads in Annetta's Travel-All at five miles an hour, or riding sure-footed horses rented from local rancheros into remote canyons. They would make camp by some abandoned rancho or near a village. Often the villagers came out one by one to stare and offer their help, showing them where sweet water flowed and instructing them in building a Mexican cookstove of mud and rocks. Usually they were accompanied by Francisco, a Loretan whom Annetta had trained as a plant explorer. At home in Loreto, Francisco fixed the car engine or the water pump, carried mail, messages, and packages from one place to another, and furnished whopping red-fleshed watermelons from his garden.

In 1964 Helen noticed alarming physical symptoms, and a year later she noted in her journal the "grim diagnosis," but did not name it. She had Parkinson's disease. With this knowledge she seemed to plunge even more enthusiastically into living. She skied, she camped, she hiked long and far, and she traveled.

There were six trips to Mexico all together, two of them deep into central Mexico to see and study art and architecture, and the other four to Baja California. In 1964 she spent over three months in the British Isles. The occasion was the International Botanical Congress in Edinburgh, where she met her old friends Flora Murray Scott, Jens Clausen of the Carnegie Institution, and California botanist Ledyard Stebbins. Before the congress she traveled and hiked in the Scottish Highlands and afterwards went to Wales, took a canal trip through Britain, and visited Ireland.

In the summer of 1966 she accompanied a Sierra Club outing to Switzerland and Austria, again hiking and climbing with strength and gusto.

The International Botanical Congress was held in Seattle in August, 1969, and Helen and Annetta drove up together. "This will be my last Congress and I will enjoy the sociability," she wrote. Immediately afterwards she retired at the age of sixty-four with a sense of accomplishment and honor. Two weeks later she was off to Europe again, this time touring Switzerland, France, Italy, Yugoslavia and Greece with Annetta and their mutual friend Florence Little.

She remained active professionally as well. In 1965 the University of California published her book, *Spring Wild Flowers of the Bay Area*. It became a best-seller among their Natural History Guide Series.

One of her last professional acts was the completion of her description of the genus *Hesperolinon*. She had traveled widely in California, especially in the north Coast Ranges, to see and collect members of this genus, and had made a careful analysis. It was her magnum opus. The work was called by Davis and Heywood in their *Principles of Plant Taxonomy*, "an outstanding example of floral morphological studies carried on in connection with a taxonomic revision."

In 1980 Nancy Morin named a harebell of the Mount Hamilton Range *Campanula sharsmithii* in Helen's honor.

Helen began to grow very thin, and Carl, Linnea, and John were shocked and saddened when in 1969 they finally learned of her illness. Helen stayed active as long as she could, kept her journal until she could no longer write legibly, saw her friends, kept up with her reading, and worked in her garden. With the advance of the disease, she kept careful notes on her condition.

As the slow, inexorable deterioration proceeded, she was put on drugs which enabled her to continue walking, but which caused mental confusion. It filled Carl with a piercing sorrow to watch her fine mind losing its way under the influence of medications he knew to be necessary.

By the end of the seventies, she could no longer manage by herself. She had stopped writing and was sinking into physical weakness and mental lethargy. Linnea came one day and found her prostrate on the floor, unable to answer the door. Linnea arranged for her to enter a rest home and to be taken off the drugs, and she began to improve.

In 1979 Linnea had entered a program in textiles at the Oakland College of Arts and Crafts and received her degree in 1980. She went on to work repairing textiles at the De Young Museum in San Francisco, at the same time giving her mother the dedicated services of cook, housekeeper, nurse, and companion. When Helen's condition worsened, Linnea left the De Young to care for her full time. Eventually Helen needed professional nursing care, and Linnea placed her in a nursing home, then negotiated for an even better location when that proved unsatisfactory. Helen spent her last months peacefully in Chaparral House, Berkeley. Carl felt a profound gratitude for Linnea's loving assistance.

When in 1982 the end came at last, he mourned deeply. The years of their separation seemed to him to have been a tragic loss. He thought with infinite nostalgia of the happy days he and Helen had shared long ago, their life in the Sierra, their mutual love, their mutual help. Having lost her once, he now lost her again with crushing finality.

He drew closer to his children and followed with interest the lives of Linnea's two sons and John's two daughters. From time to time he helped each of his children financially, having some of the joy of giving during his lifetime. He has corresponded regularly with both.

Linnea, whose training and work are in the arts, never responded athletically to the outdoors, as both her parents had. To her, the beauty of scenery and the joys of her garden suffice. She makes and repairs fine quilts for individual clients and for businesses and institutions. Though her interests are different from her father's, she feels close to him.

John early decided that botany was not for him, but studied geology and settled in Jackson Hole, Wyoming, in order to be near the mountains. He has been a ranger, done some guiding and much hiking, and become a poet, a skilled carpenter, and builder of log homes. His work with the ski patrol and mountain rescue teams as well as at his trade of carpenter keeps him in the outdoors.

Helen had hoped to revise her *Flora of the Mount Hamilton Range*, but did not live to do it. After her death Carl revised it with the help of Nobi Kurotori, and in 1982 it was republished by the California Native Plant Society.

In May, 1984, Carl went with his friends, the Harvard Medical School professors, Doctors Walter and Nan St. Goar, to Arizona. The St. Goars had been on both the Swiss and Colorado trips. Carl had looked forward to seeing the southwest again and sharing his memories with his friends. But shortly after they set out, he suffered severe chest pains: a heart attack. The St. Goars rushed him to the hospital in Nogales, from which he was transferred to San Jose, where he had surgery and spent some time recuperating.

That summer he was back in Tuolumne Meadows. His activities were greatly curtailed, and he fretted at not being able to go on long hikes and climbs as he had always done. Instead, his many friends came to visit and be with him, bringing plant specimens, cookies, and tales of their exploits. He continued to lead meadow walks for the Park Service. And he taught a week-long seminar in meadow ecology for the Yosemite Natural History Association — once again looking at nature, delving into books, and developing new lectures about his beloved mountain meadows.

When he turned eighty, he suddenly discovered that the insurance policy he had established long ago with Helen as beneficiary had matured. Although he did not want it, he was paid out a large sum of money. It was, in fact, a bitterness to him because it had never benefitted Helen. He determined to give it away in her honor. Dividing it up, he made grants of about twenty-five thousand dollars each to The Nature Conservancy, The Wilderness Society, and The California Native Plant Society. In each case, the gift was in memory of Helen Sharsmith.

28
In Sharsmith's Tent

"One life; a little gem of time between two eternities."
— Thomas Carlyle

Summer, 1985, in Tuolumne Meadows. And Carl is in his tent, the same tent he has been occupying every summer for years on end. God knows, it isn't much of a tent. On the table, a red oilcloth and a small reading light with flexible neck and metal shade. A stack of books supports an open volume he has been reading — maybe poetry, maybe geology. There are a sink, refrigerator, wood stove and woodpile, a few pans hanging on nails. Unpainted shelves hold his scanty larder: canned soup and beans, bags of potatoes and onions, plastic jars of flour, sugar, coffee, a can of tobacco, a sack of homemade soap. His easy chair, a recycled frame with worn plastic-covered cushions.

In the back room stand two iron cots with bare mattresses, a few boxes, a bar across one corner for hanging clothes, an unfinished pine dresser with brush and comb on top. The brush belonged to his mother. On his bed a sleeping bag is laid open for airing. And thereby hangs a tale.

This year, driven to it by sternest necessity, he has a new sleeping bag. He patched and mended the old one religiously for thirty years and, when he could mend no more, he bought a new one for thirty dollars in an army surplus store. He has neatly stitched in a sheet liner, then a second layer under the head, and made an invisible patch over a blemish by the zipper. The feathers from the old bag were retrieved for pillows.

No, it's not much of a tent, but it's Sharsmith's tent, and in it he holds his rustic salon. He has shrunk a little now and is slightly stooped. His parchment face is pinched into a long nose and pointed chin, and surmounted by ungreyed brown hair chopped short in a self-administered crewcut. He wears much-mended ranger pants, a voluminous grey wool shirt, and tennis shoes with leather patches. In his oversized, capable hands, an old pipe.

And because it's Sharsmith's tent, it becomes a crossroads. Hundreds pass

through in a season, thousands in a decade. Any casual visitor is dazzled by
the variety, and soon joins the multitude for coffee and talk.

One evening Nelson Nies, a healthy white-haired old Trailfinder, arrives
with his wife, all agog to tell Carl about a recent trip to Patagonia, "but there
weren't any pine trees."

Carl is mildly indignant. "Of course there weren't any pine trees! They
hardly appear in the southern hemisphere. Why, the farthest south they go is
Borneo."

For old times' sake Carl acts out the story of the mission play. First he is
the kindly padre, then squats and becomes a little Indian boy pulling the
priest's robe. Finally he takes revenge on the wicked Spanish captain, throwing an invisible sword from an invisible stage with an imperious gesture.
"There is your sword! Go follow it!" He and Nelson laugh long and hard,
and then Nelson leads him off to a prime rib dinner at Tuolumne Lodge.

Tim Palmer, river-runner, backpacker on the Pacific Crest Trail, and devoted biographer of America's wild rivers, finds his way to the tent to talk about
the Sierra, and spends a long evening, blond head bent over his notes as he
listens to Carl and learns about his mountains.

It is growing late, and a knock is heard at the open door. "Come in!" Carl
calls, then starts up to greet a burly young man. "Why, Sweet Pea, where have
you been for so long?"

Sweet Pea, a tough horsepacker, is one more of Carl's friends. They talk
late into the night about his adventures, his photography, and the flowers and
trees that Sweet Pea loves. About horses, too, and the panther with the six
foot tail he saw near Wawona, the glaciers of Alaska, the old days in the meadows, the Wind River Range in Wyoming, the Grand Canyon, the wide and
wonderful world. Carl's eyes sparkle. He listens and responds like an eager
kid.

Dee, who knew Carl when she was a child, has stayed in his tent for several
days. Now with grown children of her own, she has hiked the Muir Trail
seven times in seven summers with one Sierra Club cup, a few heat tabs, and
no tent. If it rains she rolls up her sleeping bag and sits hunched under a plastic trashbag for the night. On a cloudy morning Dee leaves to walk twenty-
two miles down to Yosemite Valley. Afterwards Carl discovers some figbars on
the shelf. "I wanted to cook her breakfast, but she wouldn't let me. If only I
had stuffed these cookies in her pocket!"

In fact, Carl never lacks for female companionship. The women who visit
him are the independent ones. "The girls nowadays are worth twice what the

Carl in 1986. Photo by Milt Irvine.

boys are," he asserts. "They've got more gumption, more get-up-and-go."
Young women rangers come by to borrow his hat for a skit or check out a
flower or a point of Yosemite history. A willowy girl in flowered skirt and soft
voice appears. Carl embraces her fondly and asks her name. "You won't
remember me," she explains, "but I'm Barbara. I was on a walk with you, and
you said if I had a question I could come see you at your tent."

"I'm so glad you've come," says Carl simply. Barbara stays for an hour talking about flowers and Shakespeare. Then he takes her for a walk in the meadow to look at the golden sedge, "which I never saw here before this year, and
suddenly it's everywhere!"

Walter and Nan St. Goar, Carl's doctor friends from Harvard, stop to pass
the time of day. Walter likes to fish, and Nan is keen on botany. Shortly afterwards Fiona from his Alaska days, now a Harvard medical student, breezes in
from a backpack with a friend, and they make French toast and everyone talks
at once.

Now Ann and Cathy appear, tired but exultant from climbing Mount
Lyell. They are faithful followers and frequent tent-visitants. At the end of
each season when the staff at the meadows leaves, Carl and Ann take a little
trip, usually east of the Sierra to look at the Great Basin flowers. He urges
Ann to drive up narrow roads into the Inyo Mountains, or lickety-split across
Nevada, and when night comes they make camp among the scented piñon

pines and junipers under the stars. One evening when it clouded over and a few drops came down, Carl laughed. "It's nothing to worry about, Ann," he murmured as they dropped off to sleep in their sleeping bags. "It's a dry rain."

Ann remembers the day Carl invited her for "a bowl of good soup," in the tent. He bustled around chopping onions and potatoes and pouring meat stock he'd saved in a jar. Soon it was done, and smelled delicious. Ann took a big spoonful. "That's funny," she thought, and pulled something hard and sharp out of her mouth. It was a nail. She slid it under the bowl and tried again. Two nails this time.

"Carl," she ventured, "there are nails in this soup."

"Really?" He dipped up a spoonful and saw it was full of nails. He puzzled a moment and then began to laugh. He giggled, he chortled, he howled until he had to wipe his eyes. "You see, Ann," he finally explained, "I had this left-over ham stock, and I poured it into a bottle I had on the shelf. Only," he had to laugh again, "the bottle was full of nails!"

A blue-eyed Cherokee woman has gone on several of Carl's Tuolumne walks. Awed and warmed by the wisdom of "The Grandfather," she gives a pipe ceremony one afternoon in his honor. Sitting among the boulders below his cabin she talks about the symbolism of the pipe, its handmade soapstone bowl, and the eagle feathers that adorn it. She stuffs it with sweet herbs, holds it up to the four cardinal directions, to the heavens and toward the earth, and says a prayer for each direction. Then she lights the pipe and passes it around the circle of friends who have gathered. Each one takes a puff and makes a silent prayer. Afterwards she talks about The Grandfather and his place in the cosmos, and gives him the eagle feathers from the pipe and some minerals in token of the ceremony. Carl thanks her with simple Indian dignity and grace.

Peter (who will spend the following summer with Carl in Switzerland), a Swiss landscape architecture student and volunteer park naturalist for the summer, produces a *Cryptantha* to be identified. A geologist brings his latest paper on glaciation. An archeologist shows an unusual obsidian point. Rangers Sarah and Ken have a new baby Carl must see — perhaps in the covert hope that he will lay upon it his wordless blessing. An official from the National Park Service asks his opinion about the preservation of the mead-ows. Art from the Merced Canyon Committee talks of the fate of the Merced River. A friendly nurse takes his pulse. An admiring photographer takes his picture. Susie gives a French horn concert.

And there are the food offerings, which arrive at Carl's tent as regularly as if he were a yellow-robed monk with a begging bowl. His food budget, already modest by habit, is minuscule because of the largesse poured upon him. Toni brings breakfast. Toby and Nobi come laden with German beer and thick steaks to cook on his old wood stove. A mysterious stranger comes bearing a five pound box of bacon-ends, one of Carl's delicacies, from Bishop. A cake or a pie materializes out of thin air, melons and peaches from the San Joaquin Valley are heaped on his refrigerator alongside a brace of trout and a loaf of homemade bread. People feed Carl, not because he is starving, but because they want to give back something for all he has given to them. And then, as Benjamin Franklin said of old mistresses, he appreciates it so much.

Thus is life in Sharsmith's tent — an ordinary ranger's tent with an extraordinary inhabitant. And in the great parade, the frankincense and myrhh of friendship offered and received, Carl's gift becomes evident. He gives himself to people with the quiet steady glow of an unquenchable flame. Others may be preoccupied, self-absorbed, careless of those around them, but Carl is open, he is there when they need him. Each question posed is pondered and answered with all his attention. Each anecdote is related as though for the first time.

Carl moves easily among human moods. A joke brings a deep prolonged belly-laugh. A sad tale can evoke a tear. He is outraged by callousness or stupidity. He is playful. On a walk among spring-green horsetails he takes a handful, cuts them into different lengths, and blows a tune like the great god Pan himself. He is Christian and pagan; he is human. "Hath not a Jew eyes?" he quotes from Shakespeare, "hath not a Jew hands, organs, dimensions, senses, affections, passions?...If you prick us, do we not bleed? If you tickle us, do we not laugh?" And in that moment he is the anguished Shylock.

Yes, he knows the world is not all good. Yet, despite an occasional grumble against times that are out of joint, he is profoundly optimistic and forward-looking. He doesn't think of death and decay, he thinks of spring and growth. He talks little of his own demise, and much of what he will do tomorrow or next year. He doesn't look at the youth around him through a long tube like a remote astronomer, but rather he borrows youth's eyes and sees each flower as though for the first time.

Where do his breadth and depth and timelessness come from? Mysteriously as mycorrhizal filaments in soil that burst into flamboyant fruiting and are said to make a forest possible, Carl has grown his personality, his tree of life, silently and richly. As a tree with spread branches, he stands with open hands giving nourishment and love to all who touch him.

29
The Sage of Tuolumne Meadows

"to hold a mountain's heartbeat in his hand."
— e.e. cummings

Time has passed...much time. Somehow, imperceptibly and irreversibly, Carl has changed. No longer the eager young ranger diffident in the presence of those older and wiser, now he is older and wiser.

When he reached seventy, mandatory retirement age in the Park Service, there was never any doubt that he would stay on at Tuolumne Meadows. He continued working summers as their senior and most-loved naturalist, almost part of the meadows. Every year they seem more beautiful to him and he feeds on them, gluts on them, draws their sweetness into him.

In 1971 he began a new career leading seminars for the Yosemite Natural History Association. For a number of summers he gave a series of five-day courses in geology, then in alpine and subalpine botany. Later he dropped the geology and concentrated on botany. This way he was able to take small groups to the high places he loved so well and to share with them in a more intense and prolonged way the distillations of his years of experience. Soon he had developed a new following — those who returned summer after summer for these demanding courses. As always, some of his students were knowledgeable in the field, others novices, but all gave themselves over to the high mountain world as they climbed to the alpine fell fields and studied their wonders.

When the Natural History Association broadened its offerings, Carl gave seminars in winter ecology in Yosemite Valley, and spring wildflower courses in the foothills. He was rounding out his own knowledge as he shared it. His fame widened like ripples in water, and the Public Broadcasting program "Over Easy" filmed his spring wildflower seminar as an example of the contributions of an unusual and outstanding "senior citizen." They didn't know he wasn't really old.

In 1981 he was the first person to receive the Yosemite Award for his fifty years of outstanding contributions to Yosemite National Park. He felt full of years now, and full of honors.

When he was young it had seemed as though, in so much time, he would have learned everything about the mountains. Now he recognizes it can never be so. He knows a great deal. He can recite the succession of blossoming like a litany. He is privy to the most secret haunts of flowers and grasses. He understands which *Erigerons* grow on granite and which on metamorphic, which mountain tops have one kind of rock cress and which another, and

The veteran ranger in 1985. NPS photo.

where the rarest species of *Arabis* are found. But he can never know it all.

For he knows, too, that this wondrous variety of the Sierra is not bounded, not finite. A little bird may bring a new seed, a mutation may occur, a storm pattern shift. Timberline moves up and down, and far above the present trees big logs remain from a warmer period; in the heart of a bog lie the bones of ancient forests.

He feels part of the mountains. Mount Lyell is a father to him, forbidding and cool, yet ultimately knowable and lovable. The Dana Plateau is a sheltering mother full of comfort and hidden wisdom. Dana Lake under its alternating winds is a child, sunshine one minute and tears the next, now calm, now spangled, and now and then when the winds meet overhead, stirred to the wildest leaps and tumbles of spray in the tossing air.

Yet no matter how close he has drawn to nature, he remains a visitor where the most delicate flower, the flimsiest bird, belongs more than a man who must have boots and jackets, ice axes and rope, and books to tell him about it. He ventures always as a loving stranger learning an alien language, and that is how it must be. It is man himself who is fragile, who is evanescent, who is ignorant, who is weak.

Within himself he can feel these things. His very life has been organic like a

tree. Before him were other trees, a forest, and behind them other forests
going back to primitive life forms. In time he was sown, a seed among seeds.
He took root, he grew as trees do, bounded by the environment he sprang
in, yet obeying an inner imperative that could seize the soil and burst the rock
and rise upward into the sun.

As a tree he was acted upon, stormed upon, struck by hardship at times.
He was also nourished and sheltered and allowed to expand.

The tree stirs in the wind. What has his life been for? He can look about
now and see the slope below from whence he came. He can feel the ripening,
the harvest. He thinks of his boyhood dreams and senses how directly he has
followed them, and how greatly they have been fulfilled. He wanted knowledge and mountains, and that is what he got.

He didn't ask for wealth. In fact, he rather abhorred it. The acquisition of
things, the pursuit of comfort, always seemed unworthy and suspect to him.
"I don't want what other people want!" he declares hotly.

Thus he has been content to live in old clothes and to mend them endless-
ly in stubborn rejection of shopping and buying. He has been satisfied with
battered frying pans and unmatched cups and a sparseness almost harsh in his
domestic arrangements, while gloating on natural beauty like a miser gloating
on gold.

Sunrise on glaciers — and a patched old sleeping bag. Boiled beans — and
an occasional slab of expensive gruyère cheese. Day-old bread — then dinner
out on the town, provided gladly by loving friends.

As evening falls in his tent in Tuolumne Meadows, he chops some kindling
and lays a fire in the stove. He gets down the blackened frying pan and starts
some bacon ends sizzling. On a board he deftly minces an onion and adds it
to the pan. Then some potatoes, a zucchini someone has given him, a bit of
cheese, and a tomato. He stirs it all together with salt and some good grinds
of pepper. "Why, it's delicious!" he announces to the empty tent. Carefully
spreading an old newspaper upside down so he won't be tempted to read
about a reprehensible world, he serves himself a hearty helping in an enamel-
ware plate and sits down to dinner.

From the books stacked on his table he selects today's choice,
Shakespeare's *All's Well that Ends Well*, and reads it slowly and reflectively,
savoring food and literature together. Then a cup of coffee, some cookies left
by an unidentified admirer when he was out walking, and a smoke.

In a nearby tent the young rangers are talking and laughing, and he feels a
moment of loneliness. The only cure is music. He straps on his twelve-bass

accordion (left behind by a fellow ranger at Tuolumne) and stands by the door looking out at the rosy glow of sunset, playing the old songs of his childhood: Swiss folk tunes, long-forgotten music-hall favorites, and themes from Mozart and Beethoven.

He can think of his life as a story without end, for it is part of the endless mountain story. He has watched bemused each season's new backpackers, some awkward and eager as birds mastering their new wings, as they roll up mint-bright sleeping bags, load unaccustomed packs, consider the merits of exotic and familiar dried foods, and walk out into the mountain world with heavy boots and light and open hearts. He knows their avidity, their joy, and he wishes them well.

He is not above deploring their ignorance, but he is there to teach them. From the distilled wonder of his many years, not diminished in age but sweet and complex as old sherry, he gives without stint. Strangers may smile at the burly and bearded young men listening with bated breath to this slight old fellow with the soft voice. Familiars don't smile, they join the circle.

What he gives them is a love of nature so cultivated, so refined, so carved by wind and shined by dew that it has become a treasure. This is his gift: watching the great show begin in the spring with the slipping away of the snow, the rise of slender stalks and the opening of delicate blossoms under a waxing mountain sun...wandering along the Tuolumne River in the brief bright halo of alpine summer, when all the *Ivesias* shine gold in the grasses, Lemmon's paintbrush washes the lawns with purple, and fledgling bluebirds learn to fly. Most of all he loves late summer when grasses head up, bilberries swell their tiny inky fruit among the sedges, golden-mantled ground squirrels hurry to fatten before winter, and humans too seem peaceful and replete under the blessing of a brilliant sky.

And like the winds across Dana Lake, all this beauty and strength and weakness and passion and wisdom are melded in the life of Carl, a small and happy man playing his accordion in the sunset of his long Sierra day.

I
Bibliography

Beatty, M. E. "Mountain Sheep Found in Lyell Glacier." *Yosemite Nature Notes,* December 1933: 110-112.

Bracelin, Mrs. H. P. "Willow Hunting in Yosemite." *Yosemite Nature Notes,* July 1933: 69-71.

Clausen, Jens. *The Harvey Monroe Hall Natural Area.* Stanford: Carnegie Institution of Washington, 1969.

Davis, William J., ed. *Trailfinders Memories.* A publication of the Trailfinders Committee, n.p., n.d.

Hough, Romeyn Beck. *American Woods.* Lowville, NY: R. B. Hough Co., 1916.

James, Harry. *Western Campfires — Reminiscences of Western Camping Over Half a Century.* Flagstaff: Northlands Press, 1973.

Jepson, Willis Lynn. *A Manual of the Flowering Plants of California.* Berkeley: University of California Press, 1963.

Muir, John. "The Hetch Hetchy Valley." *Sierra Club Bulletin*, January, 1908: 211-220.

——————. *The Mountains of California.* New York: The Century Co., 1894.

——————. *My First Summer in the Sierra.* Boston and New York: Houghton Mifflin Co., 1911.

——————. *Our National Parks.* Boston and New York: Houghton Mifflin Co., 1901.

——————. *A Thousand Mile Walk to the Gulf.* Boston and New York: Houghton Mifflin Co., 1916.

——————. *The Yosemite.* New York: The Century Co., 1912.

Munz, Phillip A. *A California Flora.* Berkeley: University of California Press, 1963.

——————. *California Mountain Wildflowers.* Berkeley: University of California Press, 1969.

O'Neill, Elizabeth S. "Walking With Carl." *Sierra*, May/June 1981: 66-69.

Ridgway, Robert. *Birds of North and Middle America*. II vols. Washington D.C.: Smithsonian Institution, 1901-1950.

Sapir, Edward. *Culture, Language and Personality*. Berkeley: University of California Press, 1949.

Schumacher, E. F. *Small is Beautiful*. New York: Harper & Row, 1973.

Sharsmith, Carl. "Comments on the Naturalist Work at Tuolumne Meadows." *Yosemite Nature Notes*, September 1931: 73-74.

——————. "A Contribution to the History of Alpine Flora of the Sierra Nevada." Unpublished PhD Thesis. University of California at Berkeley, 1940.

——————. "Glaciers of the Sierra Nevada." *Yosemite Nature Notes*, January 1932: 1-2.

——————. "New Plant Discoveries Made by the 1939 Field School." *Yosemite Nature Notes*, July 1940: 49-50.

——————. "A Report on the Status, Changes, and Comparative Ecology of Selected Back Country Meadow Areas in Yosemite National Park That Receive Heavy Visitor Use." Typewritten manuscript dated June 29, 1961.

——————. "Seasonal Progression on Mt. Dana." *Yosemite Nature Notes*, November 1933: 99-100.

Sharsmith, Helen K. *Flora of the Mount Hamilton Range of California*. Santa Clara: California Native Plant Society, 1982.

——————. *Spring Wild Flowers of the Bay Area*. Berkeley: University of California Press, 1965.

Shreve, Forest and Ira L. Wiggins. *Vegetation and Flora of the Sonoran Desert*. Stanford: Stanford University Press, 1964.

Smiley, Frank Jason. *A Report Upon the Boreal Flora of the Sierra Nevada of California*. Berkeley: University of California Press, 1921.

Starr, Walter A., Jr. *Guide to the John Muir Trail and the High Sierra Region*. San Francisco: Sierra Club, 1953.

Sudworth, George B. *Forest Trees of the Pacific Slope*. Washington, D.C., U.S. Government Printing Office, 1908.

Van Dyke, John C. *The Desert*. Salt Lake City: Peregrine Smith, 1980.

Wasmund, Erich. "Report on the Corpse-Wax in the Mountain Sheep Found in the Ice of the Lyell Glacier." *Yosemite Nature Notes*, March 1938: 45-48.

II
Ranger Naturalist Hikes & Climbs from Tuolumne Meadows in the 1950's

Key: E = Easy, M = Moderate, MS = Moderately Strenuous, S = Strenuous, VS = Very Strenuous. (Note: Full data is not available for all hikes. This list does not include short nature walks in and near Tuolumne Meadows, nor does it include hikes and climbs from other locations in the park.)

1. Bishop's Backbone.
2. Budd Lake.
3. Cathedral Lake. E. Climb 1,000'. Hike 6 mi, drive 2 mi.
4. Cathedral Peak. A rock climb.
5. Cathedral Peak, North Cirque. M. Climb 1200', drive 2 mi.
6. Children's Hike (8-10). Tuolumne's Mini-Devil's Postpile. 9:30 - 4:30. Bring lunch in knapsack, swim suit. Parents arr. transp. and pickup. Assistance of 2 parents appreciated.
7. Cloud's Rest from Tenaya Lake. S. 14 mi., climb 1800'. Drive 8 mi.
8. Mount Conness, North Peak. VS. 12,256'. Hike 10 mi, climb 2700', drive 10 mi.
9. Coxcomb Cirque: MS. Hike 8 mi, climb 1500', drive 3 mi.
10. Coxcomb Tableland. S. hike 8 mi, climb 2200'.
11. Columbia's Finger. MS. 10 mi, climb 1500'. Trail most of way. Drive 2 mi.
12. Conness Glacier. S. Hike 8 mi, climb 1500', drive 10 mi.
13. Mt. Conness. S. Hike 9 mi, climb 2400', rough going. Drive 10 mi. Summit 12,590'. (Early trips via Saddlebag Lake + Glacier; later via Slate Creek.)
14. Dana Glacier via Glacier Canyon. MS. Hike 8 mi, climb 1500', no trail and rough going. Drive 6 mi.
15. Mt. Dana. S. 13,053'. Hike 3 mi, climb 3,000'. Drive 6 mi.
16. Dana Plateau. MS. Hike 8 mi, climb 2,000', drive 6 mi. Remnant of ancient topography 60,000,000 yrs. old. View Sierra escarpment.

17. S. Echo Peak and Echo Ridge. S. 11,200'. Hike 8 mi, climb 2600', drive 2 mi.

18. Elizabeth Lake and Unicorn Peak. S. Hike 3 mi.

19. Fairview Dome. MS. Hike 4 mi, climb 1400', drive 3 mi.

20. Falls Ridge. S. Hike 9 mi. Great bald ridge between Cathedral Creek and Tuolumne River. No trail. Drive 6 mi.

21. Gaylor Lakes and Old Mines. E. Drive 6 mi.

22. Geology and Natural History Caravan. Tioga Pass and down Sierra Escarpment (Lee Vining Canyon). Mono Lake and Craters. Bathing suit for swim Mono Lake. Drive 50 mi.

23. Mt. Gibbs. S. 12,700'. Climb 3000', rough going, drive 6 mi.

24. Gibbs, Shoulder and Old Mines. MS. 11,500'. Hike 8 mi, climb 2000', drive 5 mi.

25. Glen Aulin.

26. Granite Divide between Dana and Gibbs. S. 12,500'. Hike 10 mi, climb 2800', drive 5 mi.

27. Helen Lake. S. Hike 10 mi.

28. Mt. Hoffmann via May Lake. MS. 19,921'. Hike 8 mi, climb 2000', drive 12 mi.

29. Johnson Peak. MS. 11,000'. Hike 9 mi, climb 2400'.

30. Johnson Ridge. S. 11,000'. Hike 9 mi, climb 2400'.

31. Kuna Glacier. VS. Hike 17 mi, climb 2300', drive 5 mi. No trail, rough going.

32. Kuna Lakes. M. Hike 7 mi, climb 1500', drive 5 mi.

33. Kuna Peak, North Spur. S. Hike 12 mi, climb 2800', drive 5 mi.

34. Lake of the Domes. E. Hike 6 mi, climb 1000', drive 6 mi. Lakelet in charming setting and wide vista.

35. Lee Vining Peak. MS. 11,691'. Hike 8 mi, climb 2700', drive 12 mi.

36. Lembert Dome. E. Hike 4 mi, climb 800'. Half-day.

37. Mount Lyell. S. 3 day trip.

38. Lundy Canyon and Dore Cliffs.

39. Mammoth Peak. S. 12,225'. Hike 9 mi, climb 2700', drive 5 mi.

40. Mount Maclure (usually done in connection with Mount Lyell trip)

41. Mono Pass and Golden Crown Mines. M-E. Hike 10 mi, climb 1200' on historic trail, drive 5 mi.

42. Mono Pass and Bloody Canyon (coordinated with Geology Caravan, see above.)

43. Parker Pass.

44. Parker Peak. VS. 12,850'. Hike 17 mi, climb 3200', drive 5 mi.

45. Polly Dome. E. 9,786'. Hike 6 mi, climb 1100', drive 6 mi.

46. Polly Lakes. E. Hike 6 mi, drive 6 mi.

47. Ragged Peak and Young Lakes. S. 10,900'. Hike 10 mi, climb 2000', wonderful view.

48. Shepherd's Crest. VS. Hike 14 mi, no trail.

49. Slate Creek Valley. E. Hike 6 mi, climb 800', drive 10 mi.

50. Tenaya Canyon and Slide Falls. M. Hike 7 mi, climb 1000', drive 8 mi.

51. Tenaya Peak. MS. 10,700'. Hike 9 mi, climb 2500', drive 8 mi.

52. Tioga Peak. MS. 11,532'. Hike 6 mi, climb 2000', drive 8 mi.

53. Tuolumne's Mini-Devil's Postpile. E. Hike 5 mi, drive 3 mi.

54. Tuolumne Peak. S. 10,875'. Hike 8 mi, climb 2000', drive 12 mi.

55. Unicorn Saddle. MS. Hike 7 mi, climb 2100'.

56. Mount Warren. VS. 12,337'. Hike 12 mi, climb 2837', rough going, drive 12 mi.

57. Waterwheel Falls. 1 1/2 day trip. ("Those who may desire to make the entire trip in one day may return to the Meadows late Saturday afternoon.")

58. Mount Watkins. M. Hike 8 mi, drive 14 mi.

59. White Mountain. S. 12,300'. Hike 8 mi, climb 2300', car 10 mi.

III
Index of Plants Mentioned

IV
General Index